Original title: *Fascismo Revolucionario*
 © Erik Norling, 2001.
 © Ediciones Nueva Republica, 2001.
 http://www.edicionesnuevarepublica.com

This edition: *Revolutionary Fascism*
 © Erik Norling, 2011.
 © Finis Mundi Press, 2011.

Translation: Finis Mundi Press
Proofreader: Robert Ledwidge

Finis Mundi Press
http:/finismundipress.blogspot.com

ISBN: 978-989-8336-26-2
Copyright deposit: 332372/11

A record copy of this book is available at the
Portuguese National Library.

Finis Mundi is a registered trademark of Antagonista Editora (Portugal)

Revolutionary Fascism
by Erik Norling

Finis Mundi Press

Contents

A sort of a prologue
    by Francisco Calderón 7
Benito Mussolini, the "Red" years
    by Jaime Nogueira Pinto 11
I - Nicola Bombacci, from Lenin to Mussolini 27
II - A Revolutionary Experience,
    the Italian Social Republic (1943-1945) 39
III - Long live Europe!
    Europeism and Fascism (1930-1945) 55
IV - The Black Brigades: a Party at Arms 73
V - The "Socialisers" of Italian Fascism (1922-1945) 81

Appendage

I - Separation from the Socialist Italian Party 87
II - Fascism's foundational program
    (February 23rd, 1919) 89
III - Program of the Italian Combat Fasci 91
IV - Benito Mussolini's speech
    to the Italian people (18th of September, 1943) 93
V - The Verona "Manifest" 97
VI - The Socialization,
    law of the Italian Social Republic 103
VII - Companies' Socialization Bill of Law 105
VIII - The workers and Socialization 117
IX - Speech to the "Resega" Division 119
X - The Lyrical's address 123
XI - Chronology: the 600 days of the RSI 139

Revolutionary Fascism

A sort of a prologue
Francisco Calderón[1]

I remember well the day that Juan Antonio Llopart[2] invited me to write the prologue for *Revolutionary Fascism*. That morning a funny smile settled upon my face, one that wouldn't go away until late in the evening. That had to do- as the reader can imagine – with my friend's offering, a man that has made from literary rebelness his flag; that has chosen to publish free books in a country in which one enjoys freedom... in the sole condition of not making use of it. For all of that I'm proud, tremendously proud, of being able to write a few lines as a sort of prologue for a book of *Ediciones Nueva Republica*, a publishing house that has managed to survive in the middle of the storm unclenched by the "democratic" and "tolerant" winds. May these words serve as a humble homage to this tireless fighter that humbly works for to make books like these one available to us. Thanks Juan Antonio.

Focusing ourselves on the book that we are dealing with, *Revolutionary Fascism*, we must highlight that this is its third edition [Revised and Expanded]. An objective piece of information corroborating that author Erik Norling made a magnificent work, as usual. Other than that, one rests assured that Norling always expands his investigative works, intending to offer his reader updated documents about themes that seem not to be of interest to the caste of subsidized and servile historians that abound in our times.

The two words that title this book perfectly describe its content: *Revolutionary Fascism*. The authors intentions are clear; to analyze the "revolutionary" - rupturist, transformer - component of the movement unclenched by Benito Mussolini. A necessary study, as if it is certain that Fascism was itself essentially revolutionary, the pseudo-Fascism of some reactionary movements, grouped by the official History in the same waste basket, as well as the Rightwing deviations of the Mussolinian regime, can mislead those who catch a first glimpse on the phenomenon.

---

[1] Director of *Krisis21*, official newspaper of the Spanish Republican Social Movement.
[2] The publisher of the original Spanish edition.

Erik Norling

Mussolini: from Marxism to Patriotic Socialism

There is nothing better for starting to understand the nature of Fascism than to get to know the life of its creator -Mussolini -by the hand of Jaime Nogueira [Pinto]. In his article Nogueira [Pinto] describes for us the youth of a middle class Italian, the son of an Anarchist blacksmith and of a teacher, somewhat branded by a sort of genetic revolutionary instinct. We will get to know the restive Mussolini, the Mussolini that immigrated to Switzerland to dodge the draft influenced by the ideas of his ambiance. We also shall get to know the proletarian Mussolini, working as a mason's apprentice, a butcher and as a bellboy in a chocolate factory. The Mussolini arrested for mendacity and vagabondage, sleeping underneath the bridges and dressed in rags.

Little by little we will unravel the revolutionary Mussolini, the Socialist Mussolini who read the Communist and Anarchist classics but also thinkers like Nietzsche and Sorel, which had an undeniable influence over him. We shall see how his true nature starts to conceive a patriotic feeling - unfamiliar to the Marxist discipline – a philosophy of life associated with action and creation. Therefore, already at the epoch in which he was the director of *Avanti!* (The main voice of the Italian Socialists), Mussolini starts to sway towards a rupture with the Marxist heterodoxy, rejecting the "classic dogmas" claiming that the "Socialist Revolution is an act of faith".

The break of World War I will accelerate Mussolini's metamorphosis, making him abandon the barricade of "non-interventionism" to join the warrior avant-garde calling the Italian youth to battle. The Marxist cowardice and its lack of realism lead the proletarian leader to position himself at his fatherland's side opposing the internationalist complexes of his comrades. Expelled from the Socialist Italian Party, the Fascist adventure of Mussolini begins. The time was right for the Combat Fasci, the Socialist and Nationalist slogans, the relentless fight against his former comrades, the warrior romanticism and the alliance with the Futurists. Afterwards - following good results in the elections - a brief turn to the Right that shall bear no fruits: and then the return to the radical and Socialist values of Fascism; to its essence. Next the march on Rome, again a turn towards Conservatism, and it starts all over again. Though Italian

Revolutionary Fascism

Fascism had a leftist origin, occasionally Mussolini made concessions to the Right, but it died pure, with socialist leanings, rebellious and deeply revolutionary.

The compagnons de route and the RSI

It would be ludicrous to reduce Fascism to the figure of Mussolini, as his travelling companions were much more than supporting actors. Real or authentic co-protagonists of the Fascist adventure, man like Bombacci (founder of the Italian Communism and friend of Lenin) or Pavolini (tireless paladin of the party's Leftwing) have reaffirmed the purely revolutionary character of the movement. Erik Norling, aware of the "others" importance, devotes them several chapters.

Thanks to his work we will be able to understand why a Communist like Bombacci was to join Fascism in the most difficult of times (just before the final defeat) visiting the factories, one after another, promoting Socialization. A Bombacci fateful to his ideas - to the dead - that would shout, facing his henchmen with a serene and courageous gaze, "long live Socialism!" seconds before they were to riddle him with bullets. He was not the only Leftist that embraced Fascism; Norling outlines that the regime had the support of well known Antifascists, Socialists and Communists, that saw with great expectation the [political] changes undertaken by Mussolini. People like Walter Mocchi (one of the most well known Leftwing intellectuals, a Sorelian, co-founder of the Italian Communist Party), the illustrious jurist Rolandi Ricci, philosophers like Gentile or Edmondo Cione, the Socialist Cario Silvestri (a bitter enemy of Mussolini during the Ventennio) converged and gave their definitive support to the Social Republic, in which they saw materialized their dreams of a true workers republic.

He shall likewise discover the significance of the word "Socialization", making a thorough analysis of the regime that allowed the most revolutionary Fascists to turn their ideas into practice, the Italian Social Republic. A regime vilified both by Liberals and Marxists but that constituted a breakthrough in social issues and a clear example of what Fascism could have turned out to be if it hadn´t suffered a military defeat…

not in vain "*in a few months more than eighty companies were Socialized, overall they employed about one hundred and fifty thousand workers. The property transfer policy of the workers housing was a reality (days before the end of the war houses where still being adjudicated), meanwhile the workers participation in the companies was a fact.*" Simultaneously to this revolutionary and socializing process, however, one of the most sad episodes of Italy's History was in the making; an authentic civil war between Fascists and Partisans that would serve as a prologue to the bloody end of an era, marked by the brutal prosecution of anyone who would "smell" of Fascism.

Norling also dedicates a chapter to the study of the Fascist Europeistic component, an undoubtedly revolutionary ingredient in times in which the European unity was a Utopia. A work of investigation continued in his book "*Eurofascism*"- a mandatory reading- also published by *Ediciones Nueva Republica*.

If to the aforementioned we are to add the carefully selected annexes, before our very own eyes arises an essential work, a magnificent résumé of the Italian Fascism and an "ideological weapon" of priceless value. Thanks to this book we shall realize, to what extent Fascism is, in the author's own words, "an open cosmos", a real or an authentic ideological "Big Bang", a revolution of thought that overthrows the barriers of Left and Right to aim much higher. An aim - frustrated by the conflict outcome - of finding the perfect equilibrium between the Social and the National.

Revolutionary Fascism

Benito Mussolini, the "Red" years[3]
Jaime Nogueira Pinto[4]

What a character!

In the threshold of his monumental biography on the founder of Fascism, André Brissaud posed the question, who was Benito Mussolini? : *"To some an anti-Communist Reactionary, a chaplinesc dictator, a carnival Caesar, without historical importance, an 'insignificant parenthesis' in Italy's History".*

"To others, a bold reformer, a Statesman out of the ordinary, a Roman reincarnation, a humane and heroic guide, perhaps a martyr or a saint..."

After this dichotomy, the author presents a synthesis answer: *"In reality this son of the Romagna, a Far-Left revolutionary Socialist, invented Fascism (historic truth that one must accept), and for the next twenty three years he became Italy's Duce, turning it into a European power. He was one of the most important characters of the international scenario from 1920 to 1945".* All of the intellectuals for hire, from whatever parallel, always in the market, from sponsor to sponsor, selling ideas and strategies to the Left, Right and Center, according to the buyer's taste and the daily fluctuations, will always have difficulties to seize these vital phenomena, strangers to the economicist rationalization, escaping Marx, Adam Smith, Freud and whatever *vademecum*; above all because, since its beginning, their individual and collective existence was a war without truce against the former classifications, against the simplistic dualisms, against the rules extracted from former rules.

"What a character!", was the exclamation of ironic tenderness, pronounced by Dona Rachele (which will faithfully accompany Mussolini, quiet and discreet in the glorious times, gaining a new stature with the frequent adversities, standing out, since 1945 as the family head, the Widow, the strong woman) when in 1922 the king called upon her husband

---

[3] First published in *Futuro Presente*, issue 15/16, fall 1983.

[4] Director of *Futuro Presente*, magazine of the original Portuguese New Right, member of the Heritage Foundation (Washington, USA) and of the Institute for Political Studies (Liechtenstein).

to form cabinet. "*What a character!*" One only has to review the epoch's European press, listen to his contemporaries, ("*If I was Italian, I'd be with you, I would be a fascist*" Churchill told him in Rome; "*Providential man*" Pius XI called him.) take a look at an old photo or film, listen to an epoch record, to understand the charismatic character, astoundingly popular, of this man that, in December of 1944, four months away from dead and defeat, regardless of the ghastly sufferings of the war, the misery, the bombings, in spite of the harshness of Terrorism and Counter-Terrorism, still gathered one hundred thousand persons in his last public speech in Milan…

"*What a character!*"… Accordingly to Sir Ivone Kirkpatrick, stationed in Rome during the golden years of Fascism, Mussolini's personality, the ramification between the flamboyant public figure and the awkward family man that detested mundane life, driving his own automobile and sheltering himself in Villa Torlonia with his family, corresponded to one reality: "*This lonely life that he chose and which gave him a very useful mystery aureole, corresponded, in his hearth, to his tastes. The same thing goes for his simplicity. He was not seduced by luxury. He had only interest in money in the exact measure in which it would serve his basic needs. He never indulged himself (…) titles and honors were also of no interest to him. One can understand by such that the example of austerity which he gave Italy did not suppose any personal sacrifice.*"

"Nobody understands him" - "one time shrewd, another naïf; sometimes brutal, sometimes docile; vengeful and ready to forgive; generous and petty, the most complicated and more contradictious man I have ever known" - wrote Fernando Mezzasoma, one of his companions, in the last week of their lives…

Revolutionary Fascism

The roots and the masters

Perhaps some biographic data may provide some keys to decipher this personality.

In Italy's map, in the heart of Romagna, equidistant from Florence and Bologna, near Forli, stands the village of Dovia de Predappio. There, or more exactly, in a large house in a poor conservation state, situated in a nearby hill, in a place known as Varano da Costa, was born slightly more than one hundred years ago, the son of the revolutionary Anarcho-Syndicalist blacksmith Alessandro Mussolini and of the elementary school teacher Rosa Maltoni, the future leader of Fascism. Baptized with the names of Benito, Amilcare and Andrea; Benito due to the Mexican revolutionary Benito Juarez; Amilcare and Andrea due to the Italian Anarchists Amilcare Cipriani and Andrea Costa, the later being Bakunin's secretary. A christening that is, by itself, all a political program.

Alessandro is a self-taught revolutionary, a fervent Bakuninist, founder of an International section in Predappio, present in all riots and street fights against the authorities, usually an habitué in taverns and cells for political reasons; one of those curious characters, a mix of free thinker and advanced Socialist that used to define Socialism like this: *"Science enlightening the world; reason over faith; free thinking overthrowing prejudices; free accord among men to lead a truly civilized life; true justice established on Earth, a sublime harmony of idea, thought and action".*

After a turbulent dwelling in the Faenza Salesians, where his hereditary anti-clericalism erupts violently, the young Mussolini enrolls in the School of Forlinpoli, engaging as a speaker and a journalist during his academic life, enjoying a Platonic peace, getting initiated in lesser Platonic affairs, as well as in politics.

Being renowned as a subversive and a revolutionary, the only vacancy available for Professor Benito Mussolini was in the elementary school of Piave de Saliceto, a village in Gualtieri - "Italy's reddest Commune". After a while, he decides to leave Italy and goes to Switzerland to dodge the draft. And there, the classic procession of toils and hardships of all emigrants and emigrated: hunger, humiliation, resentment, dreams of greatness and revenge. Mussolini works as an apprentice mason, as a butcher, and as a bellboy in a chocolate factory. He is detained for mendacity and vagabondage, sleeping underneath the bridges, dressed in rags, a willful and scaffold look (as we can see in photos taken in prison, when he was 20 years of age), a Karl Marx medal upon his chest would hardly make him fall in the good graces of the Swiss police.

Nevertheless in Lausanne, aided by Vilfredo Pareto, he discovers Blanqui, Kropotkin, Gustave Le Bon and above all Georges Sorel, in the library of a university. Sorel is a whole new world to the passionate young revolutionary, assiduous participant in the Nihilist and Marxist circles of the Brasserie Landolt, where Angélica Balabannoff completes his revolutionary education, with readings that ranged from the German idealists to the Utopian Socialists; and above all, Proudhon, who Mussolini will qualify as "genial".

But Sorel is his biggest discovery... Sorel's "Ethic Socialism", his "Syndicalist metaphysic", the Myth over the utopia; the heterodox, voluntaristic and Aristocratic Marxism; and all of a philosophy and action theory. *"To me, the essential is to act. But I say again that I owe the most to Sorel. It was this Syndicalist master who, with his rude theories about revolutionary tactic, contributed the most to the formation of the discipline, energy and power of the Fascist cohorts"*, he will say, in a romantic gesture, retrospectively, in 1932...

And after Sorel, Nietzsche... this force of nature, truly knows no boundaries... Nietzsche, the great Irrationalist, the great Nihilist, the great Iconoclast, the enemy of Socrates and of the Rationalist European tradition (of which Marx is, in a certain sense, a finished product). Nietzsche that the "Socialist-Fascist" Drieu de La Rochelle shall oppose to Marx in a famous text serves as an inspiration to Mussolini. *"Nietzsche marks the center of an impending return to the Ideal. Of an ideal fundamentally distinct of those in which the past generations basked in. For to understand him, a generation of free spirits shall emerge, fortified by war, by solidarity, by the grave dangers to which they have been exposed; spirits that shall be acquainted with the winds, the glaciers, the high mountains snow and that will know how to measure, with a serene gaze, all the depth of the abysses"*, he will write, afterwards, in a text whose style owes a lot to the discovered master...

Revolutionary Fascism

To Nietzschean Nihilism he adds, in this phase, a profound anti-Clericalism and anti-Christianism, thus restaging a classic scene amongst the militant Atheists of the epoch: Watch in hand, giving God five minutes to kill him. And curiously, the extremist Socialist uses Nietzschean arguments to attack Christianism *"accusing it of being the author of the fall of the Roman Empire, weakening with its ideology the resistance to the Barbarian coup"*.

The Revolutionary Socialist

Strike organizer, permanent agitator, *indomitus*, violent, his motto in this epoch was: "arresto, carcere, sfratto" (detention, prison, expulsion).

Therefore, he is labeled *persona non grata* by the Swiss authorities (very accustomed then to revolutionaries of all kinds), roving from Lausanne to Geneva; from Geneva to the French side of the Léman lake; again to Switzerland, to Zurich; afterwards to Germany; after that to Bern. In 1905 he returns to Italy to carry out his compulsory military service; the death of his mother hurts him deeply. The Mussolini family moves to Forli, where Alessandro opens a tavern. But from 1908 on, the revolutionary professor Benito Mussolini is unstoppable; in the same year he proposes matrimony to Rachele Guidi, afterwards, in the beginning of 1909, he moves to Trento to work in the newspapers of Cessare Battisti - the daily *Il Popolo* and the weekly *La Vita Trentina* and *L'Avennire del Lavoratore*. Only for a while though, since he was expelled by the Austrians, in September, due to his irredentist and Syndicalist actions.

Again in Italy, Mussolini settles in Forli and joins Rachele. He fills the position of secretary in the local federation of the Socialist Party, and also of director-editor of *La Lotta di Classe*; making one hundred and twenty liras a month, he hands 20 to the party. Those days Italy, its national unity having less than half a century - a creation of northern men and interests - together with censitary suffrage (only three million in thirty six million inhabitants could vote) and the Catholics conscious absentism, consolidated a strong and reduced bourgeois Oligarchy at the head of the economic and political power.

The Socialist Party is a petit-bourgeois Reformist party with leaders like

Filipo Thrati, Bonomi, Salvemini more devoted to a masses encadrement action than to revolutionary agitation.

In this state of affairs Mussolini will reveal himself as a leader... as written by Pietro Nenni: "*a man, Mussolini, seemed to have the power of being everywhere at the same time, attracting the revolutionary enthusiasm of the masses... He was always willing to sacrifice theory to action. His motto was 'as long as we may fight'. And, when there was no possibility whatsoever of fighting the state, he thought that we should fight among ourselves, because in doing so we would fortify our muscles and train our spirits.*"

Soon enough the clashes between the young radical and maximalist revolutionary and the leaders of his party would commence. In 1910 - birth year of his daughter Edda and of the dead of his father, Alessandro - Mussolini became famous as a speaker and polemist. In 1911 he takes part in the campaign against war in Libya, speaking at the rallies in Forli, directing the town occupation by the Socialists, pickaxe in hand, pulling out cobblestones from the streets to make barricades... "*His eloquence recalled that of Marat*", remembers Nenni that, in that moment, was a Republican leader.

The order is re-established; Mussolini is put on trial and sentenced to one year in prison, the same for Nenni. "*We spent - he writes in his memories - many hours together, locked up in our cell, playing cards, reading, making plans for the future. Our favorite author was Georges Sorel, and his contentment of parliamentary compromising and Reformism. Mussolini was not a fetishist, a Marxist fanatic. He was a Socialist by instinct and by familiar tradition; he was, above all, a rebel... A model prisoner, he found excuses for everyone and everything, indulgent with the prison's usual guests, he would justify their misdemeanors by ways of social injustice*".

In prison, Mussolini deals with translations, writes for *La Lotta di Classe* as well as letters to Rachele. In 1911 he spends Christmas behind bars: "*it was the first Christmas that we were spending apart and it was very sad. But, there were so many sad Christmases in our life! So many that my husband was always sad during the coming of the 25 of December: to ourselves baby Jesus means bad luck, he used to say.*"

In the Regio d'Emilia congress, in July of 1912, Mussolini is about to confront, for the first time, the official party line... A young man, of abrupt

Revolutionary Fascism

gestures, with a stubbled beard, his pockets full of newspapers, mended clothes, holes in his shoes... he advocates his thesis against class cooperation, stands for class struggle, the exploiter-exploited dialectics, makes the apologia of violence and armed fight... he demands the expulsion of Bissolati, Bonomi, Cabrini and Guido Prodrecca... congress endorses him with 12.556 votes, he is "*the anti-Pope of the official Socialism of Rome and Milan*", being elected for the Executive Committee... "*The entry of Benito Mussolini in the PSI's new directive team shows that it has finally taken on a good path*", stated Lenin at the occasion.

So, as by an act of magic, "*this remarkable young man, harsh, rude, impetuous, highly original*", this revolutionary "*in which the spirit of the barricades dominates Marxist discipline*" converts himself, overnight, not only in the "*most influential personality of the Socialist Party*", but also, by the first of December of 1912, in the director of *Avanti!*, the party's official press organ.

A newspaper is, as Lenin taught, much more than a newspaper; it is, above all, a collective organizer; in three months time, Mussolini, quintuples from 20,000 to 100,000 the printing of *Avanti!*

Lawsuits, trials, violence... in the coming year he founds a magazine: *Utopia*, writing in his editorial: "*the masses, having been called to participate in the quest for a new kingdom, have a lesser need to discern than to believe. In the same way that one can be a good Christian without understanding Theology, one can be a good Socialist without having read Socialism's great works. The Socialist revolution is an act of faith*".

War and intervention

Our generation sometimes underestimates the role of World War I in the end of the old world and in the birth of another. For the first time a conflict between nations became a total war (the Northerners had already succeeded in doing so in the American Civil War); the war was industrialized, democratized, massified; chemical war, generalized draft of troops as it was never witnessed before, the machine-gun, the trenches and the positional war contributed to never before imagined massacres.

This war would give birth to immense revolutions, or better still, the models inspired in the grand revolutionary ideologies will seize power; the Bolshevik triumph is the consequence of the Tsarist army's defeats; National-Socialism is the consequence of the German defeat and of the Versailles Diktat; Italian Fascism is the product of the resentment due to a "betrayed victory".

In the Ancona Congress (May 1914), Mussolini saw his leadership consecrated - in spite of the inflated oratory of Orazio Raimondo he got the freemasons out of the Socialist Party, - reinforced both his directorship of *Avanti!* and his charismatic leadership as the *indispensable man for an authentic revolutionary movement*, harvesting the strategical fruits of using a newspaper as a voice of a revolutionary spirit amongst the Italian masses. In June of 1914, the party's progress in the municipal elections will consecrate the new hard-line.

At the same time, his sentimental life is as complex and turbulent as his political life: between the exquisitely beautiful Venetian Jewess Margharita Sarfatti, art critic in *Avanti!* and the exotic Anarchist Leda Rafanelli; between the Austrian Ida Dalser and the faithful Dona Rachele, an oscillating Mussolini, shall live, maintaining at this epoch tumultuous and passionate affairs, which will have no effect in his combativeness and aggressiveness. "A man rapped in women" and/or as a Renascence Condottieri or a meridional machist, without complexes, without problems, in himself the antithesis of the "Occidental "impossible romantic passion, represented by the minstrel's love. 1914 was also the year of the liberation of nationalist passions, and above all, of the tensions and violence accumulated by the 'reactionary' and realist signatories of the Vienna Peace, more concerned with the nature of things than with ideological passions, more with History and with equilibrium than with the nationalist feelings or with the people's will. In the eve of conflict, after the Sarajevo hit, Mussolini makes a quick and prophetic analysis of what is about to happen: *"let's see things clearly. The central empires, attacking Serbia, are attacking France and England. A general conflict is hence inevitable. I am convinced that the German Socialists will follow their Emperor. The Socialist International will be scattered into pieces. The French Socialists will find in Marxism excellent reasons to think that such a war is caused by the aggression of a military power of feudal traits against a democracy that, in spite of being*

Revolutionary Fascism

bourgeois, is nevertheless progressist. You may, thus, become soldiers of the Fatherland without enduring the slightest moral scruple. I confess that I cannot blame thee. No abyss opens between the imperatives of reality and your Socialist conscience".

And as if his confider, Michele Campagna, assuming the role of Devil's advocate, would quote his anti-militarist speeches of the past, Mussolini will add to the previous, when returning to Milan in June of 1914: *"it was not the same. Then it was all about a war of aggression. This war, on the other hand, may bring Italy's deliverance. It can solve the Trieste and the Trentino problem, pulling them out from Austrian claws, country that the Irredentist Cesare Rossi taught me to consider as an enemy of freedom. And this war can, also, bring closer or unclench the revolution."*

As a political analysis for the future he could not have done better. Things would happen as such: the 28th of July, Austrian-Hungary declares war on Serbia; in Berlin, the Social-Democrats vote for the war budget and in Paris the "sacred union" spirit reigns, baptized by the murder of Jaurès. The Italian political class divides itself between the supporters of the observance of the Alliance with the Central Empires, the supporters of an intervention at the side of the Entente and the advocates of the non-intervention among whom we can find Mussolini. At the same time, the war produces a reactivation of the division inside the Right and the Left wings. As it always comes to happen when vital matters are faced with traditional or ideological dichotomies. The Nationalists, Syndicalists and Republicans, that see the war as the fulfillment and closure of the Risorgimento, launched a violent interventionist campaign. Mussolini wonders in doubt, oscillating between the historic and national reality and the ideological principles against the "bourgeois war".

In *La Voce*, Giuseppe Prezzolini challenges him in these terms: *"dear Mussolini, either dog or hare. There is still time to escape. Free yourself from that equivoque. Let your warrior soul manifest itself entirely!"*

By October 18th, 1914, Mussolini comes to a conclusion and publishes a piece in *Avanti!* - *Della neutralitá assoluta alla neutralitá attiva ed operante*[5] - which, in its substance, represents a qualitative leap towards a Socialism integrated in the "Risorgimentale" Romantic tradition, from Garibaldism

---

[5] In Italian in the original: *From absolute neutrality to active and operative neutrality.*

and Mazzinism. The Italian Socialist Party can not behave like an ostrich and has to be aware of the moment and of the historical reality. The Socialist executive responds violently, summoning up a meeting in Bologna 48 hours later. Mussolini is casted out and forced to resign the direction of *Avanti!*

He starts once again, from scratch. Within a month, he launches a new daily newspaper, *Il Popolo d'Italia*, financially and logistically supported by Filippo Naldi, owner of *Il Resto deI Carlino*, from Bologna. From this newspaper, where he will appeal mostly to the young ones (*"I call onto thee, young men of Italy, young men from the factories and from the universities, young men of age and young men in spirit, which belong to a generation chosen by fate to shape history."*) will be born the symbology and folklore characteristic of Fascism: the Arditi black flag, the skull and the dagger, a loaded revolver and a grenade in the director's desk, where books accumulate, together with papers, first proofs and newspapers. And so they start: the letters and the adherences, amongst the Socialists and the Nationalists, from Conservatives and Revolutionary Syndicalists. From Croce to Prezzolini, from Panini to D'Annunzio, from Corridoni to the Garibaldi brothers, a solidarity movement welcomes the newly converted interventionist ("The Socialist Party expels you, Italy welcomes you!"), telegraphs Prezzolini. *"As long as I have a quill in my hand and a revolver in my pocket, I fear no one. I'm strong even if I was to stand alone and precisely because I do stand alone."* - revealed Mussolini to his associates with a certain Nietzschean taste after his stormy expulsion from the PSI. In December, Fillippo Corridoni, Cesare Rossi and Alceste de Ambris invite Mussolini to join them in the Fasci d'Azione Rivoluzionaria, and in the 24th of January, 1915, thirty persons gather at Milan in the movement's foundational act.

The war against Austria declared in May 24th, 1915, (in the Summer of 1916 it will be declared against Germany), finds the Italian civilians with much enthusiasm but with a poorly prepared army, poorly armed, poorly equipped, without cadres, with terrible vehicle, artillery and healthcare deficiencies. Mussolini, volunteer, is mobilized in September, 1915, and departs to the front as a mere private. He fights and meditates about the war: *"militarism **Made in Germany** has no place in Italy. As a matter of fact*

Revolutionary Fascism

this war fought by citizenry and not by professional armies, brings an end to caste's militarism, to professional militarism. Due to militarization the huge majority of the Italian officers originate from civilian live. All junior officers cadres are filled with lieutenants and ensigns that fight and die like heroes..." He writes in his *"War Journal"*, assembling the reflections of life in the army and the mechanization of modern life, with evocations of childhood Christmases and a certain melancholy. *"Snow, cold, infinite boredom. Order, Counter-order, disorder".*

In February, 1917, Mussolini is severely injured; he spends the decisive year in all of the world's History- the Revolution advances in Russia and the "immediate peace" slogan is endorsed by the Third International preparing to accomplish the Leninist objective of "transforming the bourgeois war in civil war, in a war against bourgeoisie" - in the hospital, convalescing.

August, in Turin, a violent insurrection explodes, it is cruelly repressed: fifty dead, two hundred injured and one thousand and five hundred prisoners... but defeatism is strong in the army and the incompetence of the Italian high command contributes to reinforce it, as it was plain to see in the Caporeto disaster (40,000 dead, 90,000 injured and more than 300,000 prisoners, and that many fugitives) that in November, 1917, exposes Italy to invasion.

After Caporeto, a spirit of "national salvation" imposes itself, in need of a "Tiger" like Clemenceau, Mussolini echoes this feeling: *"We, that wanted this war, must seize power... we need frightening men. We need men that have the energy to smash everything, the courage to injure and strike without hesitation, and the more strongly the higher the culprit is. (...) We must face today a quality problem... we, young men, I am never tired of repeating it, commit a grave error: we let our youth in old men's hands".*

In October, 1918, the Veneto offensive begins, offensive that will pave the way to the Vittorio Veneto triumph and to the 4th of November armistice with the Austrians. Blow by blow, honor was saved and, in an ancestral ritual, at Milan, the multitude acclaimed the victorious soldiers in the 10th of November.

while the living celebrate, a certain melancholy invades the country... 6,000 dead, a million injured, of which 220,000 maimed, together with the financial costs, the loss of most of the merchant navy, and the desolation and deaths that the "war disasters" bring along...

The hour of victory has arrived, Mussolini speaks to the Arditi, with a dagger and a flag in hand; combatant acclaimed by the combatants. He returns late in the evening to *Il Popolo d'Italia* to write its editorial. In that Milanese Fall night, he is aware, like a few others, "that life will never be the same again."

Milan, Sunday, March 23, 1919; at the number nine of San Sepolcro square, 119 people gather at a meeting presided by the romantic and radical Ferruccio Vecchi, the programmatic basis and the style of the Fasci di Combattimento are laid out: Irredentism and Nationalist vindication; proportional universal suffrage; women's right to vote; popular referendum; dissolution of the corporations; confiscation of the assets of the religious congregations; eight hours labor journey; minimum wages; agrarian reform; workers co-management and control, these are some of the items of this "Far-Left" program that forever will be - for the revolutionary Fascist old guard - as a sort of El Dorado betrayed by the strategic demands of the conquest of the State, due to the posterior appeasement with the Conservative powers after the victory.

These combat Fasci will grow fast in the coming years, mainly among veterans and young college boys: by the end of 1920 there will be 88 units with 20,156 members, in 1921 they will be 249,036 grouped in 834 units; and by the end of 1922, when of the March on Rome, there will be 3,424 units with a membership of 299,876 but, more than a matter of number, the phenomenon will be one of quality, and above all, it will inaugurate a new style. The Milan events of April, 1919, will be a role model on this subject. By the 13th and 14th of April, Socialists demonstrators occupy most of the town, attack public offices and clash with the police.

Marinetti, the leader of the Futurists, heads to the headquarters of *Popolo d'Italia* and informs Mussolini that it would be better for him to barricate in the newspaper building and to get ready to drive out an attack from the Socialists, whose slogan is: *"we need to torch the Popolo d'Italia and hang Mussolini"*. Quickly Mussolini and Ferruccio Vecchi organize the defense; Vecchi gathers the militia's local self defense group, gathering 150 men; 300 students from the Polytechnic sent by lieutenant Chiesa, join this nucleus.

Revolutionary Fascism

By the afternoon of April 15, approximately 20,000 Socialists march towards the *Popolo d'Italia*; the Fascists armed, leaded by Vecchi, Marinetti and Pina, head out to meet them, a real street battle unleashes, with shots, bastinade and fists; the Fascists count 3 deaths and 150 wounded of all sorts; the Socialists will not publicize their losses, a lot heavier.

Vecchi and his group of Arditi decide, with some 100 men, to attack and torch the *Avanti!* in Via San Damiano as a response. And they do it, spite the opposition of the Socialists and of the troops that stand guard. Several dead, numerous wounded, the newspaper is pillaged, destroyed and torched.

Thus the "civil war" begins.

In the political forces framework, the birth of Don Sturzo's Popolari, flags the end of Catholic absentism and the first steps of Christian Democracy; on October, 1919, in the 24th Congress of the PSI, in Bologna, the Maximalist revolutionaries from the Leninist line defeat the moderated Reformists. It's a (del) revolutionary adventurism, not in touch with reality, without attendance to objective conditions, lacking any alliances. The young Gramsci, skeptical, writes in *Ordine Nuovo*, after the Giacinto Serreti victory: *"the conquest of the state by the Proletarians will only be possible when the Proletarians and the Peasants have created an institutional system able to replace the institutions of the Democratic-Parliamentary state…"*

The first Fascist Congress, in Florence, is also marked by Maximalism and revolutionarism: attacks on the Monarchy and the Vatican, a confiscation program of "war profits", a radical fiscal policy on inheritances and rents, secularization of the state, a revolutionary reform of the military institutions, paving the way to the "Nation in arms".

In the elections of November, 1919, the results favor the Extremist Socialists, who elect 156 representatives from a total of 530; to the Liberals, who get 129 seats; and to the Populists who obtain 103; to the Fascists it's a disaster.

In the heat of the Fascist defeat, the Socialists promenade in Milan - in a sort of masquerade - the coffins of Mussolini, Marinetti and D'Annunzio; Mussolini is arrested, only to be released afterwards; the year of 1919 ends for him with great desolation, in spite of the enthusiasm awakened by the Poetic-Military expedition of D'Annunzio to Fiume.

1920 is the crucial year; the Maximalist and Socialist violence frighten the middle class in the cities and the small peasants in the fields. In this way, little by little all over Italy, the Fascist squads rise as poles of resistance. Usually commanded by former militia leaders, they grow strong in the provinces, and above all in the Irredentist zones like Istria, Carso and Gorizia. On the other hand, in the confrontations between Socialists and the authorities from April 1919 to April 1920, the Socialists have 145 dead and 444 injured while the military and police forces registered about 1,000 dead and 3,000 injured. The Leftwing violence is, at the epoch, a reality.

In the Fall/Winter of 1920, the violence spreads out to all of Italy; young wolves like Ítalo Balbo and Dino Grandi rally the Fascist ranks, joining the Syndicalist and Nationalist veterans; the first organizes in Ferrara a "civic defense alliance" (a true *condotta* of violent and fearless men that spread terror among the region's Right and Left wings); Grandi, Patriot, Republican, anti-Clerical and Syndicalist, is a Nietzschean, whose influences are rooted in Prezzolini, Sorel and, above all, in D'Annunzio and in the heroic and incredible Fiume adventure, as well as in the principles of the Chart of Carnaro.

"Right Turn" and Triumph

The new Fascist wave finds its electoral confirmation in the elections of May 15th 1921. Certified Fascists enter Parliament, among them Mussolini who scores 124,918 votes in Milan and 172,491 in Bologna (he presents himself in two circles). Grandi, Balbo, De Vecchi, Bottai, Farinacci and other future hierarchs of the *Ventennio* are also elected. Choosing the places in the hemicycle, symbolically, Grandi proposes that the Fascists be seated in the far left, that they be the "Left wing's Crest". The Duce chooses the far right, to face both Socialists and Communists.

Mussolini radically changes his tactic and discourse, speaking in Parliament, he claims to be "Liberal" in economy: *"we need to abolish the Collectivist state, such as war imposed it upon us, and return to the Manchesterian state"*, making the eulogy of the General Confederation of Labor *"that has preserved itself Patriot, like Fascism"*; he stands for profound socio-labor reforms but proclaims himself to be hostile to *"every attempt of*

Revolutionary Fascism

Socialization, Statism and Collectivism"; also, the militant Atheist and free thinker gives place to a most respectful Agnostic that proclaims that *"the Latin and Imperial tradition of Rome is nowadays represented by Catholicism(...) that the sole universal idea existent today in Rome, derives from the Vatican..."*

In closing the "second Mussolini", addresses the Socialists and the Communists: *"to us, violence is neither a system, nor a sport... we are willing to disarm, if only you will do the same, first of all in your souls..."*

This speech, marking a rupture with the Revolutionary, Romantic, Marginal and nihilist post-war Fascism is a bridge to the Nationalist, Authoritarian and Conservative Fascism of the coming regime, and also in a strategical plan a respectability moderation and equilibrium chart, which nevertheless profoundly displeasing to young ones like Balbo, Grandi and Farinacci, constitutes both a tranquilizer and a Greek gift to his enemies, to whom he offers - quite simply - truce and appeasement.

These, are formally accorded in the 2nd of August, in Parliament, between Socialists and Fascists in spite of the fact that some days earlier in Sarzana in an armed ambush of a Fascist parade, the Socialists and the police had killed 20 Fascists and injured more than a 100, without having casualties of their own.

The crisis breaks out inside the movement; the Bologna, Ferrara, Cremona, Modena, Rovigo, Piacenza, Forli and Venice Fasci claim to be completely adverse to and not obliged by the pacification agreement. In this state of mind - and to celebrate the 600th anniversary of Dante's death - the Radical Fascists organize a march on Ravena, with 3,000 men in combat formation, which terrorizes the Socialists, destructing political centers and enemy headquarters.

The Rome congress in November, gathers more than 20,000 delegates on behalf of more than 250,000 members of the Fasci, whose Social-Professional representation is as follows: about 100,000 belong to the middle classes (land owners, students, merchants, civil servants, liberal professions, teachers...); as for the rest, circa 80,000 are rural workers and about 60,000 industry workers.

Mussolini and Grandi came face to face theoretically and strategically: the first defends a line that one can consider a sway to the Right, an alliance with the Nationalists and the Conservatives, of economic liberalization; the second insists in the political line of the first Fascism. But, with the big question on dispute, the appeasement, Mussolini gives in before Grandi and publicly states that the pact with the Rightwing *"belongs to the past, being nothing more than a surpassed episode".* And, to prove the reconciliation of the two men, the 2nd Congress approves the transformation of the Revolutionary Action Fasci Movement into the National Fascist Party.

Less than a year after in October 1922, the March on Rome takes place, a political military operation to seize power in which a group gifted with will, discipline, strategic unity and a action philosophy - masterfully playing with the contradictions and divisions of their enemies - will triumph over the old liberal system, incapable of containing for much longer the National and Social passions that the war and the *betrayed victory*, had brought to Italy.

Revolutionary Fascism

I
Nicola Bombacci, from Lenin to Mussolini

April 29th 1945, the main Fascist hierarchs are shot down at the hands of the Communist Partisans. Curiously among these Fascists we find Nicola Bombacci, he who was one of the most prominent characters of Italian Communism, no more no less than the founder of the Italian Communist Party (PCI), a personal friend to Lenin, whom he met[6] in the USSR during the years of the Revolution (with a capital R). Nicknamed the "Red Pope", he will finally end up as an unconditional follower of Mussolini, rallying around him in the last months of the regime. Is his life the story of a conversion or of a betrayal? Or was it, by any chance, the natural evolution of a National-Bolshevik?

A Young Revolutionary

Nicola Bombacci is born to a Catholic family (his father was a farmer, a former soldier of the Pontifical state) of Romagna, province of Forli, in October 24th 1879, scarce kilometers from Predappio, that four years later will give birth - as well - to the future founder of Fascism. A region characterized both by the harshness of its labor movement class struggle, and a peasantry grown accustomed to rebellion, a land of extreme passions. By fatherly imposition he enters the Seminar but abandons it when his progenitor dies. In 1903 he joins the anti-Clerical Socialist Party (PSI) and decides to obtain a teacher's degree in order to serve the disadvantaged classes in their struggle (again the similitude with the Duce is evident, they even got to study in the same superior school), soon enough he will devote himself, body and soul, to the Socialist Revolution. His capacity for work and organizing skills gain him the direction of several Socialist press organs, in which he will increase his power amidst the workers movement. He will even turn out to be secretary of the party's Central Committee and an MP, where he will get to know a young man, just a few years younger: Benito Mussolini, that we must not forget was the coming man of Italian

---

[6] As a member of the Italian delegation to the Comintern´s (III Communist International) Second World Congress held in 1920, in Moscow.

Socialism before he became a National-Revolutionary.[7]

Opposing the Social-Democracy soft line, Bombacci, together with Gramsci, will create the Italian Communist Party following the PSI internal fracture, again travelling in the beginning of the 1920's to the USSR to take part in the Bolshevik Revolution, where he had already been, representing the Socialist Party, having been swayed then to the cause of the Soviets. There he is befriended by Lenin himself that would say to him at a reception in the Kremlin those famous words about Mussolini: *"in Italy, comrades, in Italy there was but a Socialist able enough to lead the people through a revolutionary path, Benito Mussolini"*, soon after the Duce would lead a revolution, but a Fascist one…[8]

As a leader (Antonio Gramsci was the theorist, Bombacci the organizer) of the newly created PCI, he will turn out to be an authentic "public enemy number one of the Italian bourgeoisie that will nickname him 'the Red Pope'". He will brilliantly revalidate his MP mandate, this time in the lists of the new formation, in the meantime the Fascist squadrons started to take on the streets facing the Communist militias in bloody fights. Bombacci will vow to detain the Fascist march to power, but he would fail, from his newspapers pages he will attack Fascism with invective pleading for the defense of the Communist revolution. This is an epoch in which the Black Shirt squadristi sing irreverent songs like *"I am not afraid of Bombacci/… With Bombacci's beard we will make spazzolini* (brushes)*/ To polish Benito Mussolini's bald head"*. An epoch in which Communism sees itself immersed in numerous internal tensions and Bombacci himself polemizes with his party comrades; one of the fractious points lays precisely in the choice between Nationalism and Internationalism. Already in the Socialist Party had he displayed Nationalist tendencies, which would be an omen of his future line, as a consequence of a document protesting against D'Annunzio's action in Fiume that the party wanted to present, Bombacci rebelled and wrote about the former that he was *"perfectly and profoundly revolutionary; because D'Annunzio is a revolutionary. Lenin said it in the Moscow congress"*[9].

---

[7] Regarding the revolutionary movement prior to Fascism, see Zeev Sternhell, *The Birth of Fascist Ideology*, Princeton University Press, 1995. Where curiously only Bombacci is mentioned.

[8] On Bombacci's revolutionary trajectory there is an excellent work, *Nicola Bombacci di Mosca a Salò*, Guglielmo Salotti, Rome, Bonacci Editore, 1986.

[9] We are speaking of the taking of the Dalmatian city in 1919 by the poet-soldier Gabrielle

Revolutionary Fascism

The First Fascism

In 1922 Fascists march on the Tiber capital. Nothing can stop Mussolini from seizing power; nonetheless it will never become absolute during the regime's early years. As an MP and member of the party's Central Committee as well as in charge of its external relations, Bombacci often travels abroad. He attends the Communist International's 4th Congress representing Italy, meeting with several Bolshevik Russian leaders in the Antifascist Action Committee. With half of his life already devoted to the Proletarian cause he is not willing to yield in his commitment to take his Socialist dream into practice. Both in Parliament and in the Communist press, he becomes a fervent defendant of an Italy-USSR approach, most surely speaking in behalf and by instigation of the Moscow leaders, but using a National-Revolutionary language that causes disturbance within the party, who furthermore was already retreating in disarray since the Fascist victory. If relations were to be established with the Revolutionary Soviet State that should prove to be in the interest of Italy as a nation, also witnessing a Revolutionary process even though a Fascist one. Immediately they accuse him of being a *heretic* and ask him to correct his position. They cannot admit that a Communist demands, as Bombacci did, to *"overcome the Nation (without) destroying it, we want an even greater one, because we want a government of workers and peasants"*, Socialist and without denying the Fatherland, *"sacred and unquestionable right of every man and all group of men"*. It's the so called "Third Way" in which Fascist Revolutionary Nationalism could meet up with the Communist Revolutionary Socialism.

Bombacci is progressively sidelined within the PCI and condemned to political ostracism, nevertheless he'd continued to have contacts with some Russian leaders as with the Russian embassy for whom he worked for, and furthermore one of his sons was living in the USSR.

He sincerely believed in the Bolshevik Revolution and - unlike his Italian comrades - that the Russians had a National sense of the Revolution. Therefore he did never deny his friendship towards the USSR not even

---

D'Annunzio that has been considered by many authors as the first chapter of the Fascist revolution. Carlos Caballero, "La fascinante historia D'annunzio en firme", in *Revisión*, *Alicante*, Year 1, Vol. IV, October, 1990.

when he already had joined Fascism for good. With the definitive banishment from the party in 1927, Bombacci enters a stage that one may qualify as the *silent years* that go as far as 1936 when he launches his publishing house and homonymous magazine baptized *La Verità* (The Truth) culminating in 1943 with a progressive *conversion* to Fascism. However it's much too easy to consider that Bombacci simply joined Fascism with all his belongings as the ones who accuse him of being a *traitor* do. We will witness a slow approach process not to Fascism but to Mussolini and to the Fascist movement's Leftwing. Here Bombacci feels comfortable and among his own, in syntony with its Revolutionary conceptions, Corporativism and Social laws, of which he will say in 1928, recognizing his identification[10] that *"every postulate is a Socialist program"*.

With the above revealed we can now assert that Bombacci is not a Fascist but that he defends the regime's achievements and the figure of Mussolini. He didn't approach the Fascist Party - he never joined the National Fascist Party - in spite his of his acknowledged friendship with Mussolini, he never accepted any of the positions that were offered to him nor ever did he renegate his Communist origins. He valued his independence more. However he was convinced that the Corporative State proposed by Fascism was the most perfect realization ever, Socialism taken into practice, a superior stage to Communism. He would never camouflage his ideals; in 1936 he would write in the magazine *La Verità*, confessing his adhesion to Fascism but also to Communism:

"Fascism has made a grandiose Social Revolution. Mussolini and Lenin. Soviet and Fascist corporative state, Rome and Moscow. Several stands already taken had to be rectified; we have nothing of which to ask pardon for as both in present and past we are impelled by the same ideal: the triumph of work."[11]

---

[10] About the Fascist Leftwing see: Luca Leonello Rimbotti, *Il fascisno di sinistra. Da Piazza San Sepolcro al congresso di Verona*, Rome, Setiimo Sigillo, 1989. As well as *La Sinistra fascista. Storia di un progetto mancato*, Bologna, Il Mulino, 2000.

[11] Quoted by Arrigo Petacco, *Il comunista in camicia nera. Nicola Bombacci tra Lenin e Mussolini*, Milan, Mondadori Editori, 1996, p. 115.

Revolutionary Fascism

Meanwhile Bombacci has a long epistolary interchange with the Duce trying to influence the former Socialist in his Social politics. The greater historian of Fascism, Renzo De Felice, wrote concerning this that Bombacci has the merit of having suggested to Mussolini more than one of the measures adopted in the 1930's[12]. In one of his letters, dated July 1934, he proposes an economic autarchy program (that Mussolini would apply) that, says Bombacci to the Duce, shows his *"will to further work in what nowadays matters the most, in the interest and for the triumph of the Corporative State..."*, he does the same from the pages of his magazine where again and again he battles for autarchy to make of Italy an independent country and one capable of facing the Plutocratic powers (meaning by that the USA, but also France and England). That is why he decidedly supports the 1935 intervention in Ethiopia, not as a colonial campaign but as a prelude of the clash between the *"Proletarian"* countries (Fascist Italy would be counted among those) and the *"Capitalists"* that irremediably shall come, *"the Global Revolution (that) will re-establish the world's equilibrium"*. The Italian action would be a *"typical and unmistakable Proletarian conquest"* destined to defeat the *"Capitalist"* powers and whose experience *"must be assumed... as a fundamental datum to the colored peoples' redemption, even though under the oppression of the most terrible Capitalism"*[13].

---

[12] *Mussolini il Duce. II. Lo Stato totalitario 1936-1940*, Turin, Einaudi, 1981 (2nd edition, 1996), p. 331.

[13] The correspondence from Bombacci to Mussolini (but not the one from the Duce to the former) is partly conserved in the Italian State Central Archive (ACS) in a special in folio.

Erik Norling

Against Stalin

The period from 1936 to 1943, was a difficult one for Fascism due to the beginning of armed conflicts that preluded defeat. At the same time Bombacci deepens his ideological approach to Mussolini. Already a man roughly in his sixties, he has witnessed the failure of many of his Socialist dreams, but being an eternal idealist he is not willing to abandon the struggle for Socialism, for *"that labor of economic redemption and spiritual elevation of the Italian Proletariat that we Socialists, from the earliest hour, have initiated"*. His publishing house is an economic ruin; his biographers have left records of the hardships and difficulties that he has suffered. An opportunistic step would have sufficed him, had he integrated the *official* Fascism and he would have had all the assistance from the state apparatus at his disposal, but he didn't want to lose his independence despite the fact that, from time to time, he is obliged to accept subventions from the Ministry of Popular Culture.

Coincidentally at the same time he makes a profound reflection about his past errors engaging on a series of attacks against Russian Communism. Thus, writes Bombacci in November, 1937, the relationships between the USSR and the Democratic countries could only have one explanation that would unmask the whole subject, *"there is just one reason, frivolous, vulgar, but real: interest, money, business"* due to that this former Communist could openly declare that *"we proclaim with a clear conscience that Stalin's Bolshevik Russia has become a colony of International-Hebrew-Masonic Capitalism"*. The anti-Semitic allusion is not new in Bombacci nor in the Socialist theoreticians from the beginning of the century, as we should not forget that modern anti-Semitism had his most feverous upholders precisely among the Revolutionary doctrinaires of late 19th century when the Jew incarnated the figure of the hated Capitalist. In Bombacci one does not find a Racialist anti-Semitism but a Social one, according to the Mediterranean theories of the Jewish problem, differing from the German or French anti-Semitism.

When of the advent of the II World War, especially when it breaks in the Eastern front, Bombacci fully participates in the anti-Communist campaigns of the regime. As a Communist leader that has travelled to the

Revolutionary Fascism

USSR his voice is heard. Nevertheless, he does not renegate his ideals, but further elaborates on his thesis that Stalin and his acolytes have betrayed the Revolution. He writes numerous articles against Stalin, about the real life conditions in the so-called *Communist Paradise* and the measures adopted by the former to destroy all of the Leninist Socialism achievements. In 1943, just before the fall of Fascism, Bombacci concluded summarizing his position in a propaganda leaflet:

"Which one of the two revolutions, the Fascist or the Bolshevik, will leave its mark in the 20th century going down in History as the creator of a new order of social values at a planetary scale?

Which one of the two revolutions has solved the Agrarian problem truly interpretating the peasants desires and aspirations and the economic and Social interests of the National community?

…Rome has won!

…Materialist, semi-Barbaric Moscow, with a Totalitarian employer-state Capitalism, wants to rally in forced march (quinquennial plans) - leading its citizens to the utmost misery - the existent industrialization in countries that during the 19th century endured a bourgeois Capitalist regime process. Moscow completes the Capitalist phase.

…Rome is a rather different thing.

…Moscow, with Stalin's reform, can be institutionally portrayed as any other Parliamentary Bourgeois state. Economically, however, there is a substantial difference; while in the Bourgeois states government is formed by delegates of the Capitalist class, there government lays in the hands of the Bolshevik burocracy, a new class which in reality is worse than the Capitalist one given that in the absence of any control whatsoever it has at its own disposal the labor, the production and the life of its citizens…[14]"

---

[14] Nicola Bombacci, *I contadini nell'Italia di Mussolini*, Rome, 1943, pp. 34 a.n.

Erik Norling

The Italian Social Republic

When Mussolini is deposed in July 1943 - and rescued by the Germans a few months later - the National Fascist Party crumbles. The organic structure has vanished, the party cadres, originating from the upper classes, have massively defected to the Badoglio's government and Italy stands divided in two (While south of Rome the Allies push North). Mussolini regroups the most faithful ones, all of them comrades from the earliest hour or young enthusiasts - hardly any high rank cadre - that still believe in the Fascist Revolution and proclaims the Italian Social Republic. Immediately Fascism seems to return to its revolutionary origins and Nicola Bombacci joins the proclaimed Republic and fully supports Mussolini. His dream is to accomplish the creation of that "Workers Republic" for which both he and Mussolini had fought together for in the beginning of the century. Together with Bombacci other well known Leftwing intellectuals joined the new government as Cario Silvestri (Socialist MP and post-war defender of the Duce's memory), Edmondo Cione (Socialist philosopher that will be authorized to create a Socialist Party apart from the Republican Fascist Party), etc.

He establishes a first contact with Mussolini, an epistolary one, in the 11th of October, only one month after the proclamation of the RSI. Bombacci writes to Mussolini from Rome, a city where Fascism has clamorously crumbled down, its inhabitants having destroyed all of the former regime's publically displayed symbols, but where many still remained Fascists at heart. It is now the moment that he chooses to declare his allegiance to Mussolini. Not when all was joyful and congratulations were in order but in difficult times as only true comrades do:

"Today, more than ever, I'm totally on your side" - Bombacci reveals him - *"the king-Badoglio vile betrayal has utterly brought ruin and dishonor upon Italy but has liberated thee from the Pluto-Monarchic compromises of 22.*

Today the path is clear and as far as I am concerned one can only turn to Socialist endorsement. First of all: Military victory.

But to assure victory you must assure the support of the Proletarian masses. How? Taking decisive and radical action in the economic-productive Syndicalist sector...

Always at your service with, by now, thirty years of high esteem."

Revolutionary Fascism

Mussolini, haunted by the military situation, but more resolved than ever to take his Revolution to term, now that he has loosened himself from the past ballasts, authorizes the Party's most radical sectors to seize power and the so-called "Socialization" phase is set in train (name proposed by Bombacci and accepted by the Duce) resulting in the proclamation of clearly Socialist inspired laws regarding the creation of Syndicates, enterprises co-management, profits distribution, nationalization of crucial sectors of industry. All of this is summarized in the 18 points of the first (and only) Congress of the Republican Fascist Party in Verona, a document drawn by both Mussolini and Bombacci set out to be the basis of the Social Republican state. As for foreign policy he will try to convince Mussolini that one had to: sign a peace agreement with the USSR and carry on with the war against the Anglo-Saxon Plutocracy, resurrect the Rome-Berlin-Moscow axis of the National-Bolshevik geopolitical thinkers from the 1920's. A proposal that seems to have an effect on Mussolini who shall write several articles in the Republican press regarding the subject, even though he knew that this proposal was tenaciously opposed by a large sector of the Party, particularly Roberto Farinacci. Bombacci travels north and reinstalls himself next to his friend Walter Mocchi, another veteran Communist leader converted to Mussolinian Fascism that works for the Ministry of the Popular Culture.

If for many the last Mussolini was a broken man, a German puppet, one cannot be but surprised with the devotion that he received from men like Bombacci, a true Idealist, with a tall stature, a large beard and attractive oratory, allergic to any form of encadrement and bourgeoisism, that not even now will accept any wages or stipends (only at the beginning of 1945 shall his name appear in a appointments list of the Ministry of Economy as Head of the Unified Work and Technical Confederation). Bombacci will turn out to be Mussolini's personal assistant and confider, to once again attract the workers to join the Party's bases. He proposes the creation of Syndical committees, open to non-Fascist militants, Syndical free elections, he will travel along the industrialized Northern factories (Milan-Turin) explaining the Social Revolution of the new regime and the reasons of his allegiance to it. It seems that the old Revolutionary fighter rejuvenates once again, after a meeting in Verona and several visits to Socialized companies, he writes to the Duce in the 22nd of December, 1944: "*I have spoken one hour and a half in a conquered and enthusiastic theatre… the audience, composed mostly by workers vibrated shouting: yes, we want to fight for Italy, for the Republic, for Socialization… In the morning I have visited the Mondadori, already Socialized, I have spoken with the workers that form the Management Counsel which I have found full of enthusiasm and understanding for this mission of ours*". Meanwhile the military situation was increasingly deteriorating and the Communist terrorist groups (the tragically famous GAP) had already decided to eliminate him due to the danger that his activity brought upon their objectives.[15]

But the war is coming to an end. Benito Mussolini, counseled by the former Socialist MP Cario Silvestri and Bombacci, proposes to hand over the power to the Socialists, integrated in the National Liberation Committee, rather than to the Rightwing leaders in the South. Nevertheless they fail.[16] By April, 1945, the German military authorities surrender to the Allies, without informing the Italians, it's the end. Abandoned and alone.

---

[15] More than 50,000 Fascists will be executed by these terrorist groups along these two years and another 50,000 in the tragic Spring-Summer of 1945. They had especially in mind those Fascist leaders that had a popularity aureole and that could incarnate a more Populist face of Fascism. The most outstanding case was the one of the philosopher Giovanni Gentile, which inclusive gave place to protests even inside the same Antifascist resistance. There is a large bibliography concerning the facts, nevertheless nowadays it is being attempted to reduce the numbers and the impact of this bloody civil war.

[16] Is curious to acknowledge as in several European countries, by the end of the war, the only faithful elements to the new order are the so-called "Proletarian" wings of the National-Revolutionary movements and that the surrender of power be negotiated with the Socialist Resistance groups rather than with Communist or the Bourgeois. This shall happen in Norway, where the Syndical sectors propose a coalition government to the Social-Democrat Resistance in April, 1945, or in France where after the Marshall Petain's cabinet fall in the Autumn, 1944, Marcel Déat and Jacques Doriot struggle to establish a Socialist government.

Revolutionary Fascism

A National-Revolutionary Crepuscule

During the last months of the RSI, Bombacci continued, even then, the campaign to recuperate the popular masses to keep them from leaning towards Bolshevism. In a pamphlet titled *This Is Bolshevism*, published in late 1944, reproduced in the Catholic newspaper *Crociata Itálica* in March 1945, Bombacci insists in the criticism of the Stalinist deviations from Real Communism that have destroyed Europe's true Revolutionary Syndicalism due to Russian interferences. In these last weeks of life of the Republican experience Bombacci stands with those that still believe that a compromise solution with the enemy is possible, thus avoiding the country's ruin. Loyal to the end he will remain with Mussolini even when all is already definitively lost; prophetically he speaks of this to his workers in one of his last public appearances, the 14th of March, 1945:

"Brethren in faith and struggle... I have not renegade my ideals for which I have struggled and for which, if it is God's will to grant me the possibility to live a while longer, I will always fight for. But now I do stand in the ranks of those colors upholding the Italian Social Republic, and I address thee once again because time is upon us and it is truly crucial to reclaim the workers' rights..."

Nicola Bombacci, always faithful, always serene, will accompany Mussolini in his last and dramatic journey to his dead. In April 25th he is in Milan. The testimony from Vittorio Mussolini, a son of the Duce, of his last meeting with his father, at that time accompanied by Bombacci, show us the interiness of the last.

"I thought about this man's fate, a true Proletarian's apostle, once a bitter enemy of Fascism and now standing beside my father, without any position or stipend, faithful to two different leaders to the death. His calmness comforted me." [17]

---

[17] *La vida con mi padre*, Madrid, Ediciones Cid, 1958, p. 267.

Erik Norling

Shortly after Mussolini had parted ways with his last faithful column to spare them of having to share his destiny, Bombacci is arrested by a band of Communist Partisans along with a group of Fascist hierarchs. In the morning of April 28th he faced the firing squad in Dongo, in the Northern part of the country, by his side was Barracu, a valorous veteran, mutilated by war; Pavolini, the Party's secretary-poet; Valerio Zerbino, an intellectual and Copolla, another thinker. All cried out before the firing squad that assassinated them: "*Long live Italy!*", whereas, a paradox in itself and a faithful reflex of Nicola Bombacci's controversial personality, he, as his body fell riddled by the bullets of the Communists, would cry: "*Long live Socialism!*".

II
A Revolutionary Experience, the Italian Social Republic 1943-1945

As denigrated, inclusive by those who declare themselves to be the heirs of Fascism, as unknown, the last phase of Italian Fascism developed an intense radicalization in its National-Revolutionary postulates. An experience that was carried into practice originating some hopeful results, scaring some Marxist sectors of the Antifascist Resistance due to its achievements obtained in solely twenty months of Republican-Social Fascist government.

The Italian Social Republic is born

In July, 1943, Mussolini is deposed by the Fascist Grand Council and arrested. Meanwhile the Fascist hierarchs, the military high commands and the Royal Household negotiate with the Anglo-American Allies to put an end to the hostilities and switch sides. To many it's the end of the Fascist *Ventennio* that had started in the early 1920's transforming Italy in a modern and industrialized country. With the monarch's agreement a military man- Marshall Badoglio- is nominated to head the government, in an attempt to pull out the country from the profound crisis in which several years of war had plunged it: allied troops in Italian soil, the country converted in a battlefield and a large part of the public opinion demoralized. In all of Italy the symbols of Fascism are destroyed, the headquarters of the Fascist National Party are raided by the mob; the Party cadres shred their membership cards and go into hiding, afraid of reprisals. Overnight a regime that had enjoyed a wide Social consensus vanishes, without any opposition, none whatsoever. September 8th Badoglio announces a unilateral armistice with the Allies, the war is over so do believe all of those that have commemorated the downfall of Fascism, likewise the army crumbles and the soldiers simply lay down their arms and go home. The tragedy of September 8th initiated in the 25th of July was the corollary of a dramatic material and moral earthquake in the very foundations of the Italian nation. Drained by years of struggle, discouraged and frightened, lacking a leader, the Italians jump to the pit. The Allied troops already occupy the Southern half of the country, only a few kilometers away from Rome. Nevertheless many are the Fascists that wish to remain faithful to their ideals, to their compromise to the German ally, to the Duce. For them the 8th of September was a dark day, one of National mourning, of dishonor, that must be amended. The torch's flame must be kept alight, one cannot betray the principles for which so many Italians have been sacrificed; it's imperious that Mussolini returns to lead the Black Legions in a reconquest of the country. They are the other side of a conflict that is giving birth to a bloody civil war. The Italian Social Republic is born out of this climate.

Bearing in mind the necessity to recover Mussolini, the Germans rescue and liberate him in the 12th of September. At the 18th he addresses the Italians in a radiophonic speech, there are many still in doubt but the most faithful ones receive him with a wave of popular enthusiasm. The Duce returns to take the reins of Italy - of the Northern zone that hasn't been occupied by the Anglo-American troops - and to place himself at the head of a cabinet to restore Italy's honor and do its outmost to avoid the hardships that the bellicose situation brings upon the civilian population. On September the 15th, Mussolini had once more met with Hitler, in that meeting, the former convinces him (he was considering withdrawing from public life) that he must return to Italy because if not Germany would have no other choice than to treat the country as a battlefield and as an occupied nation like some of his collaborators demand of him. Mussolini has no way out. He confides to his son Vittorio: *"there is no other way: it is necessary to rescue Italy from greater disasters."*

Obviously Hitler considers the overthrowing of Mussolini almost as a personal insult. But first and foremost he has conscience of his organizational skills and he knows that his leadership may serve to avoid Italy's plunge into chaos that would allow the Allies to push forward more rapidly towards the continent. The Italians and Germans fierce resistance in the Italic peninsula, that the Allies never could break, will show that Hitler was not mistaken. Mussolini's dilemma, and his decision to assume the head of the new Republican Fascism, is one of the Duce's life chapters that

Revolutionary Fascism

shall contribute the most to boost his myth among the posterior generations of Fascists. Mussolini didn't abandon his faithful ones when he could. Nor did he betray them, and, the most important of all, done it solely and exclusively for the love of the fatherland. The most reputed historian of Fascism, unsuspected of a Fascist past, the Italian Renzo de Felice, wrote "*Mussolini, whether we like or not, accepted Hitler's project by Patriotism: a true sacrifice in the altar of Italy's defense. Not due to a whish of vengeance... nor by political ambition... all had already vanished. Mussolini returned to power to serve the fatherland.*"

The moral situation in which the Fascists find themselves at - first of all Mussolini - is one of a clear collapse. They believe that the time for defeat has come and they feel ashamed if only to comment what has happened. A disdain that they breed in the air each time they must deal with the Germans. Badoglio's defection provoked a cataclysm in the Italian National feeling, even amongst the Antifascists that was considered as an insult to the fatherland´s honor, and Fascism's credibility suffered considerably. Even in countries so akin of Italian Fascism, like Spain, the overthrow and posterior armistice was considered to be the end for Mussolini. In Franquist Spain the iron censorship permitted the publication, in 1943, of a book by a Spanish correspondent in Italy, Ismael Herraiz, that caused a commotion and of which several editions were printed, titled *Italy, out of combat*, which could forebode a similar change in Spain.[18]

Immediately afterwards the Duce decrees five brief orders of the day that are simultaneously made public. Firstly he announces that he assumes, once again, the supreme leadership of Fascism; secondly he nominates Alessandro Pavolini as secretary of the Republican Fascist Party; thirdly he commands all authorities, both military as civilians, to reassume their positions, including the ones that may have been destituted by Badoglio; fourthly he declares that he shall rebuild the Party, support the German army in his fight against the Allies, assist the people and procure an exemplar punishment for the traitors; in the fifth and last order of the day he reorganizes the Volunteers Militia for the National Security (MVSN) that is to say the Party's militia. He immediately reconstructs the party, re-baptizing it Fascist Republican Party, in only a few weeks 250,000 militants

---

[18] *Italia fuera de combate*, Madrid, Ediciones Atlas, 1944 (8th edition).

enroll, a number that show us the broad affection that Mussolini's figure aroused in the Italian people, even more so if one bears in mind that a few weeks earlier his images were being destroyed in the streets and all seemed to be lost. He was conscious that he couldn't trust in the former Party hierarchies (Church, Patronage, Army and Aristocracy) that formerly, in the Fascist *Ventennio* had been so diligently beside him and that in a matter of days had revealed themselves as traitors. Due to this he surrounds himself with new and enthusiastic cadres, most of them Fascist veteran "old shirts" that had been relegated by the opportunists during those years to organizations like the Syndical or the youth wings where they were thought to be in no position to "hinder" the traditional powers. Meanwhile the state administration and the Armed Forces are reorganized; the later now in a popular and political army model (700,000 men will pass through the ranks). In a few months Mussolini had succeeded once again to bring a defeated Italy back to its feet, filling his militants with hope.[19]

---

[19] Nothing or little has been written about the Italian Social Republic outside Italy; for the Castilian readers we recommend, although they are but memoirs, nevertheless very well documented, the work of that who would become an MSI senator, Bruno Spampanato, *El último Mussolini*, Ediciones Destino, Barcelona, 1957. For works of a more Academic tone, in Italian: *La Reppublica Sociale Italiana 1943-1945*, VA, Fondazione Luigi Micheletti, Brescia, 1986; Franco Massobrio and Umberto Guglielmotti, *Storia della Reppublica Sociale Italiana*, CEN, Roma, 1978.

Revolutionary Fascism

Italy - Republic - Socialization!

Disappointed by his unambiguous failure in attempting to attract the Conservative strata of society (Church - Army - Patronage) Mussolini doesn't hesitate even for a second and returns to his Socialist origins, accompanied by his earliest hour comrades that had swore allegiance to Fascism due to its National and Social penchant. Not in vain primeval Fascism was considered as a Radical-Syndicalist reaction before it was neutralized. Facing a group of old Milanese Fascist veterans, Mussolini announces his proclamation, basis of the new Proletarian and Syndical new state that he desires to build:

"Some still ask of us: what do you want? We answer with three words that summon up our entire program. Here they are… Italy, Republic, Socialization.
…Socialization is no other than the implantation of an Italian Socialism, humane, ours and possible; and I say 'ours', as it makes of work the sole cornerstone of economy, casting away the mechanical leverages non-existent in Nature and impossible in History.[20]*"*

All of this could be found in the famous "Verona Manifest" where the party had celebrated his first and only congress, in November of 1943. Read by Pavolini, the party's general secretary and fervent supporter of the radical line, and written by the Duce himself, the 18 points that constitute it are all a plea in favor of a Workers' Republic, with a definitive triumph over of Capitalism - returning to the co-management of the companies by the workers - and an exaltation of the National feeling that should serve as a basis for the drawing up of a future Constitution of the Republic. As it was to be expected the Manifest was assumed with hope by the most radical and Revolutionary sectors of the Party, while the most Conservative saw with displeasement the increase of influence by the Syndicalists and Revolutionaries around Mussolini. Republican Fascism doesn't resemble at all the one experienced in Italy a few years earlier, and it was, as said by the

---

[20] Mussolini addressing Milanese Fascists and Black Brigade "resega" officers, October 14, 1944, Op. Cit, Spampanato, pp. 682-683.

Italian researcher of the phenomenon, Luca L. Rimbotti, *"since the earliest hour, a will to overcome the gradualist and conditioned Ventennio's policy to resolutely solve the problem's core."*

The RSI will turn out to be, much more than during the Ventennio, a true intent to create, *by politicizing it*, a state built upon a Social and Revolutionary ideology. At the occasion the Fascist Party will not display the same totalitarian traits, nevertheless the war's evolution along with the imposing of Revolutionary measures from its own political program and the militarization of its supporters as a consequence of the civil war experienced by Italy in those months turns the Republican Fascist Party into the backbone of the last Mussolini's whole history. Likewise, the first and only Republican Fascist Party Congress, in Verona, is essential for one to succeed in having a complete vision of the RSI's posterior politics, as such we will dedicate a special attention to this event that shall mark one before and one after in Fascism's ideology, we may very well consider that the basis of the modern Neo-Fascist ideology are laid out in Verona, and that until this very same day these ones continue to be present in Italy, represented by several political parties.

Among the first measures dictated by Mussolini in the 15th of September was the nomination of Alessandro Pavolini as, provisionally the order says, Secretary of the new Party *"that from this day on will be known as Republican Fascist Party"*. Immediately several of the Fascist federations in the free zone, that is to say the one not occupied by the Allies, reopen the Party headquarters that had stayed shut during that summer's confuse journeys. There are numerous testimonies of confusion and incertitude reigning at first, soon to be transformed in a fanatical and passionate political activism. Federations are set up in almost every city, led by Fascist militants that elect their ruling bodies in improvised assemblies until directives start to come in from the general secretariat. Accordingly with Romualdi's reminiscences, he that shall turn out to be the Party's vice-secretary and member of the National Directorate during this period, the Party was rapidly reconstituted:

Revolutionary Fascism

"Between the 15th and 30th of September, one can say that the resettling of the Fascist activity in the territory from Naples to Bolzano was absolute. The adherences, very modest in the earliest days, will reach in the coming months the remarkable figure of circa half a million enrolled…

The federation that saw the greater number of adherences was Rome with 35,000 enrolled. Followed by Milan with 20,000, and Ferrara that after the Ghisellini crime sees its members rampage in a matter of three days from an already remarkable figure of 8,000 to 14,000; next came Venice, Turin and Genova".

It's interesting to outline the Party's quick growth. In two months' time it will have 250,000 affiliates reaching almost half a million in 1944 in a moment where prudence was in order for the large majority of the population. The Antifascist Resistance parties had the same problem, they also couldn't count with support and militantism from the general population, like in all conflicts about 90% preferred the easiest solution. In percentage terms the RFP would encadre more than 3% of the population, which is a very high figure (one should bear in mind that the National Socialist Party had only 0.9% when it rose to power in 1933) and even more so in those circumstances when Partisan reprisals were in order against the families of those that dared to publicly display their Fascist allegiance.

We already saw how Pavolini had moved to Rome in September to reorganize the Party and recruit some well know figures for the new government. In Rome he nominates a provisional directorate that shall act like the Party's central organ, and orders the Party to resume its activities. The definitive directorate of the Republican Fascist Party will only be nominated in January 22nd 1944, when the Duce approves its composition. At its head we shall find men who have Pavolini's absolute trust in charge of the various Party services: regional delegates, delegates for the occupied territories (Southern zone clandestine Fascism), youth wings, delegate for external relations, the Veterans National Association, fallen for the Fascist cause, national volunteers, etc.

On the 28th of October 1943, a great assembly of militants of the new Party is held in Rome. In the capital, with less than four weeks of existence, the Party had already enrolled over 10,000 members. The old files from the

Fascist National Party where not used for the new formation given that many of its members were now in the Allies side and due to the desire of the new Fascist leaders to create a new militant base. The assembly - that ends with a public demonstration headed by federale Bardi in Colorína square, in front of the Party's headquarters - gathers more than 4,000 Fascist militants. As the German military intelligence services reveal in the very same day, the demonstration caused astonishment because the ambiance experienced at the time in the eternal city was one of strained expectation - waiting for the Allies to enter the city – to see as thousands of Fascists made a public profession of faith, after having lived the summer bitter journey, when they were persecuted by the mob that had taken into the streets, furthermore convinced the Roman population, which in its large majority stood aside from any political activity, that the end of the war was not so close as one could first have thought.

The first large public demonstration, of a transcendent national level, that should serve to draw up the program of the Party on the making will be held in Verona. It would be the first congress of the Republican Fascist Party and it had as a primary goal the discussion of the new Republican Constitution, the first step to call upon a constitutive legislative assembly that would lay the foundations for the new state. To the congress would attend the new provincial leaders, a few provincial governors and members of cabinet. The Duce was to preside to the RFP's congress.

In the 14th of November the congress gathered, baptized as *I^a Assemblea Nazionale del P.F.R.*, in the Northern city of Verona, at the main hall, the Music Room, of Castelvecchio, the town's fortress. Union and Party delegates participated, representing the about two thousand affiliated members. A wide space, decorated with old Fascist lictors and a sole flag, the one of the Social Republic to the right of the presidency's table. Outside the delegates await their entry; a mix of Squadristi and military, workers and civil servants, with various uniforms, weapons strapped to their belts and carrying machineguns gave a special ambiance to the congress, the only common trait being the black shirt. Many of them were veterans from the primeval Fascism that responded to the Duce's call in this new phase, others were youngsters with the desire to re-enact those myths. Presents were Ricci, the commander of the militia; the minister of Justice, Pisenti; the

Revolutionary Fascism

minister of Public Works, Romano; the Corporative Economy one, Gay; the Verona province leader, Cosmin and others. The congress lasted only one day, distributed in two sessions: one in the morning and the other in the afternoon with interventions from the delegates and the approval of all the order of the day points.

Alessandro Pavolini presided to the assembly, in civilian clothes but with a black shirt (he will not use uniforms regularly 'till the summer of 1944). The congress opened with the reading of a message from Mussolini who could not be present (actually he wished that the Party were to attain its independence from the state and to have the myth about his person debunked, already proven useless when of the Badoglio coup). The Duce pleaded the need for the Fascist militants, "*at arms once again*", to defend the Social Republic giving it an authentic Revolutionary meaning like primitive Fascism had done. "*It is time to start over. All that we [Fascists] are left with is a strong will accompanied by a dogmatic faith...*" in this moment in which "*all is dispersed, destructed, lost*".

Afterwards the secretary-general Pavolini read the main address; in it the terrorism question was a major issue. To many of the participants that was a daily pressing matter: to defend their families and comrades from the Terrorist attacks. That being so the Party declared war without quarter against the Partisans, "*without leniency*" said Pavolini, as the firsts had declared against the Fascists. He states, however, that the Party's organization should, from now on, be based in the quality of its members and not in number like it had happened in the past, passing on to the most transcendent point of the day: the Verona Manifest.

This National-Revolutionary policy could have remained a mere propaganda effect or ideological speculation but the Republican Fascist government takes action immediately. In the 30th of January, 1944, a few months after the Verona Congress, the Basic Law preliminary to the Socialization Law is promulgated, "*fundamental premise for the creation of the new Italian economic structure*", which is materialized in the Socialization Executive Order approved by the cabinet council in the 12th of February of that same year. Within this law we may find principles like the co-management of the companies, nationalization of those [companies] required to the development of the national economy, distribution of profits, etc.

Erik Norling

One of the main aspects characteristic of the new Fascist phase is the affiliation of recognized Antifascists, Socialists and Communists, that welcomed with great expectation the turn taken by Mussolini. Therefore characters like Walter Mocchi (one of the most outspoken Leftwing intellectuals, Sorelian, co-founder of the Italian Communist Party), Nicola Bombacci (the 1920s Italian bourgeoisie "Red Pope", Lenin's personal friend and founder of the Italian Communist Party), the reputed jurisconsult Rolandi Ricci, philosophers like Gentile or Edmondo Cione, the Socialist Cario Silvestri (devoted enemy of Mussolini during the *Ventennio*), converged and gave their definitive support to the Social Republic, in which they saw materialized their dreams of a true Workers' Republic.

The Workers with Mussolini

The endorsement that the RSI received cannot be understood if not for the intense Social Revolution that was being taken into practice, attracting numerous elements from the Leftwing that converged to the ranks of the new Fascist Party. But we must not forget that in Italy the revolutionary tradition was especially rooted in the workers circles and that the Fascist Socialization wasn't but a natural evolution of a National-Revolutionary conception of society that existed in Italy since the beginning of the century, as the Israeli historian Zeev Sternhell[21] clearly demonstrated.

The reaction to the reform was immediate, and indeed it made an impression upon the workers, even though in the post-war attempts have been made to belittle those effects. In many factories orders of the day were voted, meetings were held and motions approved. Co-management was a fact. More than 80 companies were socialized in a few months; altogether they employed about 150,000 workers. The ownership transfer policy of the workers living quarters was a reality (days before the end of the war living quarters were still being adjudicated) while the workers participation in the companies was a fact. And all of that bearing in mind as Spampanato tells us, *"the industrials passive resistance, seconded by general engineer Leyers,*

---

[21] *The Birth of Fascist Ideology: From Cultural Rebellion to Political Revolution*, Princeton University Press; New edition (3 July 1995). Spanish edition: *El nacimiento de la ideología fascista*, Siglo XXI Editores, Madrid, 1994). Perhaps the most profound and serious study on the Proletarian origins of Italian Fascism.

Revolutionary Fascism

the war economy German intendant in Italy, which in good faith feared eventual economical disturbances." This opposition from the Capitalist classes and German authorities, always reluctant as to any sort of experiment that could interfere with their war effort, was rallied by the strategy of the Socialist and Communist Antifascists who saw their main propaganda premises assumed by the Fascists. We are not taken by surprise by the Terrorist group's blood thirst, attacking Syndical leaders and grassroots Fascist militants, subscribing a strange alliance with the Italian patronage, now their travelling companions, with the support of the Catholic Church to sabotage the Socialization. Therefore, one of the post-war measures of the new government will be the annulment of the Socialization law that had inclusive received favorable critics from the Socialist and Communist Party's national leadership. After the war no few Fascist Syndical leaders will return to the ranks of the class Syndicates.[22]

The war is about to come to an end, Mussolini and his Social Republic have only four months of life left, the sectors that support him are the most disfavored: the Workers. In all of the factories he is asked to go ahead with the Social reforms, to carry out the Revolution, while the squads of the Black Brigades witness the arrival of thousands of volunteers to its ranks, willing and able to sacrifice themselves for the Mussolinian Social revolution. Mussolini's words in his last and improvised grand public rally are eloquent. These were delivered in December the 16th, 1944 -in the Milanese lyric theatre - before a multitude of tens of thousands of Fascists, originating from all corners of the city having heard the news that he was to speak there. In the street the Fascists pile and they most follow the speech through the loud speakers, listening for one last time to their Duce in what has been considered the political will of the Duce of Fascism. Between applauses and acclamations, reminiscing about Socialization, Mussolini says:

---

[22] The work of the Italian Pietro Neglie, *Fratelli in camicia nera. Comunisti I fascisti dal Corporativism alla CGIL (1928-1948)*, Mulino, Boulogne, 1996, is an excellent exposition of this tendency. No wonder that the MSI, heir of the Republican Fascism, and a true political force in Italy 'till its dissolution in 1995, has always struggled between the "Left" and the "Right" wings, the last one triumphed, giving birth to Fini's National Alliance, nowadays integrated in the Rightwing party of Silvio Berlusconi.

"*After the last events we are willing to give a new impulse and outreach to action both in the Political and Social fields.*

In reality, more than a new stand one should say more precisely: a return to the original positions... but, now, the seed has been sown. No matter what may occur, this seed is destined to germinate... the Fascist Socialization is the logical and rational solution that avoids, the economy's burocratization through a state Totalitarianism in one hand, overcoming the Liberal economy's individualism by the other... it must be considered today as a solution meeting the demands of the National communities Social traits.[23]"

Mussolini, a Communist? One can never accuse him of such, in fact he will oppose them with the same firmness that he used against Capitalism, but like to many other well known National-Revolutionaries of the epoch, as Drieu la Rochelle in France or Montero Díaz in Spain, the Communist solution was preferable than to see their countries immerged in the Anglo-American Pluto-Capitalist current: "*tomorrow, the Italians will have to chose a master. In the certainty of this eventuality, I, as an Italian citizen, would not hesitate even for a moment to chose Stalin... Today, Stalin is in a position to do what Hitler was unable to do but could have done with positive results.*"[24]

The Civil War

The saddest aspect of the RSI period was precisely the specter of Civil War, never accepted by the *Resistancialist* historians - as the notorious Italian historian Renzo de Felice baptized them - that conceal it as a *Liberation War* against the German occupier and its Italian *accomplices* (the Fascists). The truth is of a very different kind. It was an authentic civil war, with the suffering, blood and dishonor that it brings. Partisans against Fascists, Italians against Italians, that took place between September 1943

---

[23] Rep. in *Storia della Reppublica Sociale Italiana*, Massobrio & Guglielmotti, pp. 1120 to 1151.
[24] Quoted in *La agonía de Mussolini*, Giovanni Dolfin, AHR, Barcelona, 1955, pp. 253-255. Personal secretary of Mussolini in a given stage of the RSI, his testimony is in general tilted by an excessively anti-German and pro-Conservative vision.

Revolutionary Fascism

and May 1945, aside the other dispute that was taking place on Italian soil, World War II and the clash between the Axis and the Allies. The best study made on the Italian civil war is authored by the Italian historian Giorgio Pisano deceased (1997), that with his encyclopaedical work *Storia della guerra civile in Italia* has shown all the horror of a brothers conflict by ideological reasons, provoked by interests alien to Italy. We can't forget that this war is triggered by the Communists when, having received orders from Moscow, they had to avoid at all cost the consolidation of the RSI's revolutionary experience. The Italian Communist leader Togliatti launched the slogan, from Radio Moscow, to all the Communist militants in Italy: "*Death to the German invaders!; Death to the fatherland's traitors!*" Identical slogans are broadcasted by the Allied radiophonic services from the South: "*Eliminate the Fascists!*" It will be a struggle without quarrel. Provocations, reprisals, massacres from both sides, but with a clear horror supremacy in the war carried out by the Communists. Above all one must seed terror, provoke the Fascists getting them to react in a similar way and by so getting the civilian population - about 90% of which were non-belligerents, only interested in getting over it the best they could - involved.

The assassination of Gentile, senator, president of the Italian Academy, moderate intellectual personality, strange to all hate, that had given his endorsement to the RSI by conviction and because he was to make his bid for the National reconciliation, marks a before and an afterwards in the civil war. The Florentine philosopher, considered as an international eminence, is shot down by the Communists on the 5th of April 1944. His family pleads the Fascists that no more reprisals be undertaken. His assassination is immediately condemned – absolutely not called for – inclusively by Antifascist personalities that sum themselves to the mourning, causing the Communists to divulge the version that the Fascists had assassinated him. His execution is to all a symbol of the civil war. But he is not the only one. The Fascist were being victimized by assaults for months now, like the assassination of Ferrara's popular *federale*, Igino Ghisellini, shot down by the Communist *gapistas* when he was driving back to his house in November 1943, his death caused a group of Fascists to vindicate him assassinating, by their turn, eleven well known Antifascist town personalities. From Ghisellini to Gentile, the assassinations of Fascists and others affiliated to the RSI can only be explained by the intent, attained, of the Italian Communist Party to consolidate itself as a military force able to oppose the Fascists. The PCI was an insignificant party and only the civil war made possible for it to grow sufficiently as to convert itself in the Italian Left hegemonic party during decades in the post-war.

On December 28th 1943, the seven brothers Cervi were shot at the hands of the Guardia Nazionale Republicana after their complicity with the Partisan actions in their region, Reggio Emilia, had been demonstrated. This episode has been converted in the maximal symbol of the cruelty of the civil war and of the Fascists, according to the official historiography. However nobody remembers the, also seven, brothers Govoni from Pieve di Cento (Bologna) - among them a woman - that in the 11th of May, 1945 - when the fight was over and the whole of Italy was occupied by the Allies, were massacred by a Communist gang after being horribly tortured and mutilated. The Fascists took the bitter end in these two images of the same civil war. Another dramatic and cruel episode of the civil war was the famous assault of the Roman Via Rasella in March, 1944, when a German police column - made of bolzanos, that is to say Italians of German ethnicity - was defenseless massacred in Rome at the hands of the *gapistas*. Furthermore, in the assault died several civilians including an innocent child. The 33 Bolzano policeman - all too old to be able to serve in first line military units were avenged, according to the strict normative of the International Law by the execution of 335 hostages in the Ardeatine Pits. This episode has given place to several films praising the Communist action, making a legend out of it when all was but a savage assault that made no sense whatsoever other than to provoke German reprisals. All of this having in mind that Rome was considered an open city, where no military actions could take place. The Ardeatine Pits tragedy, and that of the attack, regained its actuality in the middle of the 1990's when the German Erich Priebke, aide of Rome's chief of security - extradited from Argentine - was prosecuted in Italy. The Germans - usually not at all that interested in the developments of the Italian brotherly war - would only react if German personnel were to be targeted in the attacks, like the one in Via Rasella. Their reprisals and hostage executions were always more selective than the ones of the RSI that were always made in the heat of the moment.

Revolutionary Fascism

The episode of the taking of Florence is equally relevant for one to understand the intensity of this fratricide war. Florence, as Rome, had been declared an open city to preserve it from the struggle. This was abided neither by the Allies - that will bomb it - nor by the Communists that will use it to their terrorist attacks. In August the 8th British Army closes in on the city. To delay the Allied offensive the bridges are blown away while the German units retreat from the city, followed by the bulk of the Republican authorities and units. However about 400 Fascists decide to remain in the city occupying neuralgic points to protect the retreat and the civil population. Only the intervention of these courageous fighters will prevent the Communists from taking the city before the Allies and thus provoking a blood bath as was expected.

Pavolini personally ordered the constitution of these units of Fascist volunteers, among them there were about 80 feminine auxiliaries. Distributed in groups from two to three members, to each one of those was assigned a position. If they could no longer resist they would successively fall back. In the 8th of August the Communist divisions were closing in on the city and the Fascists opposed a fierce resistance. In one of these confrontations fell the Communist commander "Potente" - the *Amo's* leader- consequence of a mortar round. After several days of vacillations, finally the Communist leadership determined the 11th as the day appointed to take the town. The Fascist's resistance impressed the attackers, *"youngsters fanatized by the Salô's Social demagogy"* said some Antifascists in order to explain the valor and bravery of these volunteers. The fight was carried out from one house to another, against snipers placed in every window and roof, backed by some German sections. Between the 15th and the 18th of August the Germans ordered the definitive evacuation of the city but the Fascists decided to stay, in a desperate fight. When the Allies entered the city in the 31st of August, some Fascists cells were still resisting. The battle will finally end in the 2nd of September when the last Fascists are confined and shot.

The account of the - then - Antifascist writer Curzio Malaparte, in his novel *The Skin* - where he narrates in a biographic tone his experience in the American side - about these Fascists valor is revealing. He describes the arrival to Florence, just occupied by the Allies. There he views a Dantesc scene; he will witness the execution of young Fascists – in the staircase of Santa María Novella's Church- at the hands of the Communist Partisans. Even facing death they will uphold their honor motto. They were but *"youngsters... Fascists from 15 to 16 years old, loose hair and broad forehead, black and sparkling eyes in their paled faces... there was also a young girl, almost a child, among them..."* reminisces Malaparte. The Communist commander pointed out one of those youngsters and said: *"it's your turn. What's your name?"* to which the Black Shirt answered with contempt: *"today it's my turn, but one of these days it will be yours."* Soon after the youngster would cry *"Long live Mussolini!"* while the Communist bullets were piercing him. Their sacrifice has made possible that even today the RSI fighters saga be remembered while the one from the Partisans is a theme that one would rather forget.

The civil war will proceed in its bloody course even after the end of the war, and it will leave behind it a stele of almost 200,000 dead. One of the most bloody domestic wars witnessed by Western Europe, only to be overcome by the Spanish one of 1936-1939, followed by the French in 1943-1945 where 105,000 Frenchmen died at the hands of their compatriots.

The End of a Dream

By the end of April 1945, war is coming to an end. The Germans negotiate with the Allies, while in Berlin the Russians are about to destroy the Reich's capital. The most radical Fascists ask Mussolini to resist, not to follow the Germans in their defeat, because they still have large zones of the country that haven't been taken by the Allies. With a column of faithful ones he travels north but all is finished. Mussolini is murdered as well as the Fascist leaders; all over the country the *Fascist hunting* unclenches, with the Allied troops -that were supposed to uphold the order - connivance.

Republican Fascism was ended, but the ideals that they had fought for hadn't died out and, contrasting with Germany and other countries, in Italy the former Fascists will reorganize without more ado and soon after they will be back in politics. The MSI (*Movimento Sociale Italiano*[25]) was born.

---

[25] Italian Social Movement.

III
Long live Europe!
Europeism and Fascism (1930-1945)

One of the most Revolutionary aspects of Fascisms, specially the German form, was its conception of Europe. For the first time, wide sections of the European population believed in the possibility of overcoming the National plan and in the march towards European unity. This gave rise to a very intense debate indeed, much broader than we commonly believe nowadays. One which was not limited to the intellectual strata, thanks to the war propaganda it spread out to encompass the common people paving the way for what was to become the post-war European Economic Community. All throughout the *New Order's* Europe preconized by the Third Reich, proposals were discussed and elaborated about the continent's future reconstruction after a military victory, not only in those years when victory seemed to be at hand (1940-1943) but also in the worst moments when all were but setbacks (1944-1945).[26] This debate also had to occur in Italy, birthplace of Fascism, being strongly intensified during the tumultuous months of the Social Republic.

An ideal that can be personified by those young Fascist volunteers, that cried out "*Long live Europe!*" while being shot by the enemy.

When Dreaming was Possible, the Ventennio, 1922-1943

The European Fascism myth is not born (nor surely does it die) in the years of the World War II. One must remember the Pan-Europeistic sway by some Fascist intellectuals during the 1930's, featuring characters with the stature of Asvero Gravelli, Pellizzi, Evola, that then had scarce influence in the doctrinal construction of Fascism but that after the war will emerge as the true spiritual guides of a new generation of neo-Fascists.

In its Europeistic vision this primeval Fascism conjugated such elements as: validity of the Fascist doctrine as a universal panacea, 19th century reassessment of the concept of nation, corporativistic ideas that necessarily

---

[26] H.W. Neulen, *Europa und das 3. Reich*, Munich, Universitas Verlag, 1987.

included an economic reordination of the continent together with a desire to make the eulogy of Rome's myth as being the predecessor of the Imperial European idea[27].

In October of 1922, Benito Mussolini, founder and soul of the Fascist movement, was appointed as Italy's prime-minister following the famous *March on Rome*. So begun the lengthy ruling period of Italian Fascism, it would last until 1945 and along with it came the chance to put to use the state's resources to promote and divulge a totalitarian ideology that had inspired the Fascist *squadristi* in their struggle for power. From the first moment Fascism characterized itself essentially as a Nationalist ideology, among other aspects, that being such in its first stage Mussolini refused any possibility of *exporting* Fascism, something that he would maintain inclusively until the early 1930's when he replied to a journalist's question - inquiring if it was possible or not to export Fascism -with a blunt answer: *"No sir, not to any country. It is an Italian product"*[28]. This position was in accordance with the times; Italy was experiencing an epoch of *national reconstruction* in which Fascism was absorbed in the resolution of the internal problems, having scarce expansionist inclinations in foreign matters. This didn't prevent that Fascism, as such, was to be seen as a revolutionary ideology able to be presented as a doctrine of universal reach, capable of overcoming the ideologies in vigor 'till the moment, assuming a redemptive nature as a whole. By 1925, in the movement's official ideological magazine *Gerarchia*, Mussolini himself had declared that *"possibly not before long, a great part of Europe will be sort of Fascist"* and the Fascist great council had discussed the possibility of forming a kind of *Fascist International*, that was never taken to term. To this added the immense echo and heartfelt empathy that the Fascist revolution had caused in the rest of the world, due to that soon enough, throughout the entire West, intellectual and political currents started to emerge claiming the possibility of putting to use those positive aspects to solve the internal problems of their own countries. Many historians have already dealt with

---

[27] Dino, Confrancesco, "Il mito europeo del fascismo (1939-1945)," in *Storia Contemporanea*, Il Mulino, Boulogne, February 1983, year XIV, n° 1, pp. 5-45.

[28] Emil Ludwig, *Talks with Mussolini*, 1933. Spanish edition: *Mussolini, Conversaciones con Emil Ludwig*, Barcelona, Ed. Juventud, 1932, p. 158. Interview made in April, 1932.

Revolutionary Fascism

this chapter of the Fascist irradiation in the pre-belligerent period of Mussolini's government and we shall not address it more than to add that this idyllic image of Fascist Italy, a Socially pacified and prosperous country, contributed enormously to divulge the notice on Fascism as an ideology capable of overcoming the contradictions in which both Liberalism and Marxism were involved. The proliferation of empathy declarations towards Mussolini and his way of government, inclusively from ambiances with a large parliamentary political tradition as England and from circles of Liberal intellectuals, constitute a good example of that.

The Fascist Evolution towards the Ideological Expansion Abroad

By the time of the 10th anniversary of the March on Rome that occurred in 1932, concurring with the overcoming of the main internal problems, when of the Fascist state stabilization, one can monitor the fast evolution of the regime's propaganda towards the possibility of an external diffusion of Fascism. This external projection will be endorsed by Mussolini's very own will. As professor Ismael Saz properly outlined, this change of heart can be somewhat explained by the Duce's mounting empathy towards the younger groups of Fascism that advocated its international diffusion as part of that redemptive mission that it contained, and also to some extent, because it contributed to the development of his external politics plans of which he was overtly found (?) of.[29] Furthermore, one can add the internationalist and modern conception of the Mussolinian thought, that, let us not forget, proceeded from the ranks of Revolutionary Syndicalism having drank from the fountains of Internationalist Socialism. He did not perceive this revolution as circumscripted solely to the Italian people but he used concepts as generic - and internationalist - as Man, Nation, Mankind, Universality.[30]

---

[29] See Ismael Saz Campos, *Mussolini contra la II República*, Valencia, Ed. Alfons El Magnànim, 1986, pp 124-125.

[30] See Benito Mussolini, *Escritos y discursos*, Barcelona, Bosch, 1935, pp. 69-102, tomo VIII, precisely found in the Italian encyclopaedia Treccani under the entry "Fascism" where this cultural background from the Duce's part is recognized. About the revolutionary origins of Fascism see the Israeli professor Zeev Sternhell et al excellent study *The birth of Fascist ideology*.

Erik Norling

Fascism's idea of ideological expansion and the doctrinal concept of *Universal Fascism* began to gestate as a current in Italy in the late 1920's, in diverse publications directed by young intellectuals linked to the regime.[31] Among these stand out Guiseppe Bottai, Camillo Pellizzi, Carlo Emilo Ferri, Asvero Gravelli with their publications *Crítica Fascista, Universalità Fascista, Ottobre, Antieuropa*, etc., that started what Italian professor Dino Confrancesco has defined as a semi-public debate on the *European myth of Fascism*. A clear evolution of the Ultranationalist postulates professed by the ideology that had nourished primeval Fascism. A theme, the one about the surpassing of the national state and of European unity through the Roman way, will achieve great success in several intellectual sectors in view of Europe's new era where the ideal of European unity divulged by the German propagandists was to be converted into an essential element of the European Fascist ideology up to the point that the post-war neo-Fascism will be first of all Europeistic.[32]

Giuseppe Bottai, founder in 1923 of one of Fascism's official magazines, *Crítica Fascista*, is one of the most influential ideologues of the party.[33] From the early beginning Camilo Pellizzi will collaborate closely with him, as Bottai he was a journalist and one of the pioneers in the debut of the expression "*Universal Fascism*" in 1925. Both of them will call for the internal renovation of Fascism in order to carry out the Fascist revolution, its universal projection could prove to be the adequate instrument in achieving Mankind's spiritual revolution as an end, along with the reconnaissance of Italy's role in this redemptive mission. The same trend is followed by the Milanese Cario Emilio Ferri, director of the magazine *Universalità Italiana* and also of the pioneering *Centro di Studi Internazionali sul Fascismo*.

After enumerating some of the early intellectuals of *Universal Fascism* we must take a look at the most notorious advocate of the Fascist universality idea as a doctrine: Asvero Gravelli. Young and passionate

---

[31] Michael Arthur Ledeen, *L'Internazionale Fascista*, Bari, Laterza, 1973. A pioneer work in which the juvenile aspect of Fascism, that chooses Internationalism, is outlined.

[32] Confrancesco, *Il mito europeo del fascismo (1939-1945)*, in "Storia Contemporanea", Bologna, Il Mulino, n° 1, year XIV, February, 1983, pp. 5-45.

[33] On Bottai and the other Fascist leaders mentioned, see Marco Innocenti, *I Gerarchia del fascismo*, Milan, Mursia, 1992.

Revolutionary Fascism

journalist with a militant record no less interesting: earliest hour Fascist in the Fascio of Milan, Gravelli took part, with D'Annunzio, in the Fiume's odyssey in 1919 being less than 20 years old, he was one of the first leaders of the Fascist youths and Bianchi's, a member of the first Quadrumviri, secretary. Furthermore he founded numerous magazines and publishing houses.[34] His toil in favor of Universal Fascism fully starts in the pages of his magazine *Antieuropa*, founded in 1928 closely followed by the biweekly *Ottobre*, founded in 1932 as a homage to the 10th anniversary of the March on Rome. In a few months *Ottobre* will be converted into a diary specially aimed at the party's juvenile sector. Its subtitle was *Quotidiano del Fascismo Universale*, the same as *Antieuropa* that defined itself as *Rassegna universale del Fascismo*. Gravelli will have a fundamental role in the early stage of the ideological elaboration of Universal Fascism. Beginning with the institutionalization of its projection, trough the CAUR, circa 1934-35 - as we shall see later on - his Europeistic vision will be defeated by those that interpret Universal Fascism as a mere projection of *the Roman way*. His position within the regime will not grant him the possibility to have an influence that one may consider as decisive and he can do no other than to watch as an outsider as his interpretation of Universal Fascism is transformed and manipulated into a mere Nationalist defense of Roman culture, that is to say Italian, with the exaltation of Universal Rome's myth.

As we have already seen, it's in the 1930's that the idea of Universal Fascism is assumed by Mussolini himself, having declared in October of 1930 that Fascism *"as an idea, a doctrine and a realization, its universal"*.[35] With explicit support from the Duce, soon the Universal Fascism current starts to be institutionally shaped thanks to the creation of study centers (as the Milanese center of Ferri) or international congresses (the 1932's in Volta is the most famous). This change in attitude will be noticed mainly in the evolution of the guidelines for the Fascist regime propaganda apparatus, which will do its best to divulge Fascism internationally and to propagate its universalistic character borrowing from the myth of Rome. Various

---

[34] See Davide Sabatini, *LÍnternazionale di Mussolini. La diffusione del fascismo in Europa nel progetto di Asvero Gravelli*, Rome, Edizioni Tusculum, no date mentioned (even though it was published in 1998).

[35] Speech presented to the federal governors, 27th October, 1930, quoted in Asvero Gravelli, *Panfascismo*, Rome, Nuova Europa, 1935, p. 59.

organizations and public or semi-public institutions are created or potentiated, to divulge the Fascist propaganda abroad. Therefore we may find the *Fasci all'Estero*, the Dante Alhigeri Society, the *Casas d'Italia* in the main capitals of the world, Italian press agencies and from 1933 onwards the Action Committees for Roman Universalism, known as CAUR.

From this moment on, coincidently dating from the celebrations paying homage to the Fascist government's 10th anniversary, in 1932, begins the second phase of the Fascist ideological expansion - this time directed abroad - one that shall not be consolidated until the Spanish Civil War, after the conquest of Ethiopia. This second period will be characterized by the abandonment of the Universal Fascism conception as an ongoing ideological elaboration only to be used, from now on, as a foreign policy instrument for Fascist Italy in its intent to stand as a first degree power. Therefore first it will compete with the emergent National-Socialist Germany, ending up afterwards by getting involved in several armed conflicts (Ethiopia, Spain, World War II) that will show the failure of this expansionist policy, provoking the intellectual decay of the very own concept of Universal Fascism. It will die out being replaced by the one of the *European New Order* headed this time by Germany, in the break of World War II. The *Myth of Rome* will be swallowed by another more attractive myth that will lay the foundations of the post-war neo-Fascist ideology: the *Myth of Europe*.

Universalistic Ideological Principles of Fascism

Pan-Fascism or Universal Fascism was an ideological concept elaborated outside of the usual forums of the Fascist movement's intellectuals, exception made for the debate that one can witness in the *Crítica Fascista* magazine. Mussolini himself and the other Fascism thinkers will dedicate but a few words to this idea, so it is difficult to characterize or locate the Universalistic ideological principles in early Fascism. It is plain to see that the journalist Asvero Gravelli seminal works contain, in good measure, the basic parameters around which the Universal Fascist propaganda will be developed. To study his prolific legacy can help us to understand the subsequent political expansion of the organizations that assume the

Revolutionary Fascism

Universal Fascism diffusion role.

His monthly magazine *Antieuropa* initiated the ideological elaboration of the Universal Fascism doctrine since an early date as we already saw. The magazine title itself was indicative, contradictory and polemical, a characteristic of the epoch's Italian Vanguardists: it was intended to break away with *old Europe*, decadent and bourgeois in the eyes of the revolutionary idealists, to impose a *new Europe* where the spiritual principles of the Fascist revolution would reign. Europe as an ideal conception will be one of the most significant components of Gravelli's and his circle of early Universal Fascists. In 1932 he will publish a brief essay titled *Difesa dall'Europa e funzione antieuropea del fascismo* that reclaimed the Europeistic component of Fascism, opposing those that would outline its Latin or Italian penchant:

"On the other hand there is an Europeism that tends to the reestablishment of the Western civilization and to a Unitarian revival of Europe... and for that [purpose] we, Italians, possess the spirit of our land and a synthesis of Europe that has the virtue of being a universal ideal." [36]

The spiritual and social crisis that threatens Europe is palpable in the early 1930's and for that it is indispensable, writes Gravelli, that Fascism assumes its role as Europe's redemptive ideology:

"We are the heresy of modern Europe... we shall establish the religious unity of Europe in order to setup a return to the ideals. Fascism, as the idea embodying modern and classical Italy reestablishes a civilization: Rome, the action's moral center... the Fascist Revolution shall be the most creative and historical of all. The Black Shirt Anti-Europe will be an idea of redemption and of unity." [37]

---

[36] Gravelli, *Difesa dall'Europa e funzione antieuropea del fascismo*, Rome, Nuova Europa, 1932, p. 21.
[37] Ibid, p. 53-55.

To achieve this double objective, the revolution by one hand and the consequent overthrow of the Demo-Liberal state by the other, the concept of Universal Fascism must be propagated at all levels, inspiring similar movements in other countries and organizing a Fascist International that could facilitate its reception by the akin sectors willing to endorse this change in attitude and in civilization. Let us not forget that Gravelli is above all a journalist and a propagandist. It is of no little consequence that Fascism had succeeded in its first revolutionary experience in Italy, now time is ripe for the remaining countries, for Fascism as an ideology has overcame its Nationalist stage. Consequently, Gravelli considers that:

"Fascism must serve to the European Fascist elements as a revolutionary tactical model to establish in more matured countries movements akin to our own, because Fascism today is no longer only an Italian phenomenon."[38]

As for the idea of a Fascist International, already at such an earlier date as 1931, he writes about it, using a vocabulary that will be very similar to the one of the Europeistic ideal propagandists during World War II. We must bear in mind that is not in vain that Gravelli will end the conflict as a member of the European Waffen SS propaganda services with the rank of SS commander. In it he will conjugate innovative elements, such as youth, Internationalism, Europeism:

"The Fascist international alliance it's the superior form of organizing the European juvenile Fascist forces... the Fascist and European youth must be able not only of destroying the old world but furthermore to construct and create a new European and universal entity... the Fascist international organization... will be the effective mean to amplify and maintain the European dictatorship of Fascism. It's all about taking the spirit of the Fascist revolution to Europe."[39]

However, with the official institutionalization, through the CAUR, of the Universal Fascism external projection, the doctrinal elaboration of Asvero Gravelli gradually lost influence. This happened while he was deepening his

---

[38] Gravelli, *Verso l'Internazionale fascista*, Rome, Nuova Europa, 1932, p. 225.
[39] Ibid p. 226-227.

Revolutionary Fascism

Europeistic vision of Universal Fascism, with fundamental titles as *Europa, con noi!* (1933) or *Panfascismo* (1935), but when the *Sottosegretariato per la Stampa e Propaganda* was structured he found himself outside the power circles. This ministry, at first a sub-secretariat, was the true organ of diffusion of the regime's propaganda since 1934 and it firmly conducted all Fascist displays. From the moment on when Gravelli is set aside, an interpretational change of Universal Fascism becomes clear, progressively it will be transformed in a *Roman Universalism* spiritually centered in Rome, from whence the new civilitá is projected.

This conception of Universal Fascism was not new; in fact it was Latinicity that had attracted the first sympathizers of Fascism from countries with Romance languages, like Ernesto Giménez Caballero in Spain. The change in the Italian external policy, which then was initiating an expansionist stage, contributed to potentiate this vision. Italy, *Roma Universale*, should be converted in the West's central axis. That being such, the elaboration of a doctrine so as to sustain that kind of aspirations was immediate. In fact Mussolini himself seems to be the main supporter of that interpretation when in March of 1934 he pronounces the famous speech to the regime's second quinquennial assembly, that Asvero Gravelli named *"the most important document on the assertion of Fascism's universality"*. The Duce said then that:

"From 1929 to the present day Fascism an Italian phenomenon at first has been converted into a Universal one... in a decade Europe will be Fascist or Fascisticized! There is but a way of overcoming the antithesis of what tells civilization apart: the doctrine and wisdom of Rome." [40]

The creation of CAUR or *Comitati d'Azione per la Universalità di Roma* in the summer of 1933 was a faithful exponent of this new line of performance. It is yet another manifestation of that much more Conservative and Catholic drift that was being shaped among the theorists of Fascist propaganda. Much more Conservative and nationalist than the one that Gravelli had imprinted upon it, much closer - as we already saw - to Vanguardist and Revolutionary positions. It is no casualness that the first

---

[40] Quoted in Gravelli, *Panfascismo*, Rome, Nuova Europa, 1935, pp. 61-53.

work published by the Committees president, general Eugenio Coselschi, would be titled *Universalità del Fascismo* even though it would constitute nonetheless just an intent to assimilate the concepts of Universal Fascism and Universal Rome, in his publication both concepts entwine and are converted into synonyms, something that did not happen with Gravelli that clearly distinguished the importance of differentiating them. This is how Coselschi interprets the notion of Universal Fascism:

"It's the name of the past and of the present.
It's the name of the future and of the eternal.
It's the name of the church and of the Empire.
It is ROME".[41]

The order of the day adopted in the first, and only, congress of the CAUR in Montreux (Switzerland) in December, 1934, *"On the universality of Fascism"* follows the same trend, given it a more Conservative, less Revolutionary, character. It is eloquent and sums up this conception main characteristics that they were to embrace (the bold Italic was printed in Italic in the original):

"a) Considering that Fascism, the political, economical and social theory created by Mussolini's genius, has become a phenomenon of a **universal** *nature, having by the strength of its principles and of its achievements imposed itself to the nations longing for youth and regeneration,* **the Montreux congress confirms the universality of Fascism.**

b) Considering that Fascism sets up a new order that so as to maintain and reorganize the moral, spiritual, familiar and national discipline necessary to the people, restricts the individual in order for him to excel on behalf of a superior ideal...

c) Considering that Fascism is essentially a revolutionary movement... **the congress reaffirms the revolutionary and constructive spirit of Fascism, the sole doctrine capable of leading the workers' world all the way through the welfare path."**[42]

---

[41] *Universalità del fascismo*, Florence, 1933, p. 14, quoted by Ledeen, op. cit. 124.
[42] CAUR, Notiziario n° 24, 23 XII, 1934, p. 6, the Congress of Montreux.

Revolutionary Fascism

From the resolution adopted one can deduce the main aspects that integrate Universal Fascism: totalitarianism, universalism and revolutionary spirit, meanwhile the Mussolini personality cult that until then was not excessively displayed in the Fascist propaganda, witnesses a crescendo. The CAUR's publications and the rest of the regime's external propaganda apparatus deliberately strived to promote the cult of Mussolini; we can interpretate this as part of its evolution as a consequence of the necessity to compete with German propaganda. To German racism they opposed *Latinity*, to the Führer, the Duce.

Hitler's rise to power in 1933 and his pre-war successful foreign policy had Fascist Italy to lose its hegemonic role as a redemptive and revolutionary power having to compete with National Socialist Germany. The Italian propaganda from the middle 30's clearly manifests this new situation. For the propagandists of Universal Fascism keeping the distance from the National Socialist ideals was imperative. They will not overtly manifest it, given that among the adherents to their committees there are many that sympathize with Hitler's rising Germany, nevertheless they will not invite National Socialist groups to participate in the meetings of the CAUR, alleging the supposed impartiality of the projected International. In the Coordinator Commission meetings records - thus of a restricted and confidential nature allowing more sensitive themes to be addressed in it - one can observe a reiterated critic to the National Socialist theories, especially to its conception of Race and to anti-Semitism. This was very common among the Italian theorists; Gravelli had also pointed it out years before.[43]

By 1935, in the Amsterdam meeting of the Fascist movements integrated in the CAUR Coordinator's Commission, a controversy broke out between the Nordic and the Meridional participants. Coselschi will have to intervene, visibly annoyed, clearly stating Universal Fascism's position regarding the Race subject. In this allocution the general would inclusively proceed to personally attack the Racialist theories of the Third Reich minister Alfred Rosenberg, author of one of National Socialism's most emblematic ideological works. We are referring to *The Myth of the Twentieth Century*, although this clearly shows yet again the lack of

---

[43] Gravelli, *Europa con noi!*, Rome, Nuova Europa, 1933, p. 129 and next.

practical knowledge that Italians had of the situation inside Germany. There it was of common knowledge that Rosenberg only had a virtual influence, - his theories having a very limited diffusion scope - however abroad he seemed to be the maximal exponent of German racism due to the anti-Nazi propaganda. This intervention from its maximal leader sums up yet again CAUR's abiding guidelines and its essential differences from National Socialist ideology:

"The exaggeration of Race cannot conduct to one Universal idea... as I see it, Fascism's universality and the intransigent conception of Race cannot be compatible. Better said, universality in the Fascist sense, in the sense manifested in Montreux, means European cooperation...

...by the contrary, universality in the Racist sense, as it is the conception, if not of all of Germany, at least of its official theorist Rosenberg, cannot exist...

If Universal Fascism truly wants to be universal and if it wants to safeguard peace it must advocate its belief in the cooperation between the peoples [of the world] and the different European races and civilizations...

As I have said this Racist question will always prevent German Fascism from being a Universal force..."[44]

In the following meeting of the Coordination Commission, in September of the same year, again in Montreux, Coselschi returns to the subject, introducing a nuance at the occasion, added to clarify the differences between both ideologies, according to him National Socialism is anti-Christian, and for that:

"We have profound differences regarding National Socialism that have been clearly stated in the Montreux congress, for example we do not have such an intransigent conception of race, and we do not fight against religion."[45]

---

[44] Coselschi, records from the meeting of the Commission pour l'Entente du Fascisme Universel, Amsterdam, 25-III, 1935, reproduced by Gisella Longo in "Storia Contemporanea", Boulogne, 1996, n° 3, June, titled *I tentative per la constituzione di un internazionale fascista: gli incontro di Amsterdam e di Montreux attraverso I verbali delle riunioni*, pp. 475-576.

[45] Coselschi, Montreux 11-IX, 1935, reproduced in op. cit., p. 559.

Revolutionary Fascism

The same came to pass on the Jewish question. A consensus was reached from the very start to avoid it in the 1934 Montreux congress; the subject would not be addressed due to the presence of well known anti-Semitic personalities as representatives of national parties. Nevertheless in the meeting held in the same place almost a year after Coselschi, as usual, will clearly state the CAUR's and the Universal Fascist position on the subject to end any further equivoques, given the insistence by some members to invite anti-Semitic groups. These would not be a part of the Entente, due to the fact that they were so far off the Fascist ideology:

"We have defined in Montreux our position concerning anti-Semitism. For us it's not a matter of Races... I think that we should invite [only] the parties that have a constructive ideal and that wish for Corporatism."[46]

The Latinicity character that impregnated Universal Fascism from this moment on contributed to the CAUR's and Universal Fascist propagandists decay in the countries outside the Latin orbit. It is obvious that other factors also played a role, but this one was important to psychologically understand the drifting apart of many well known intellectuals that before had declared themselves Fascists and that will turn out to embrace National Socialism. This applies to such important personalities as Quisling in Norway or Mussert in Holland having left evidences of their incommodity about this trait, manifesting it inclusively in the meetings of the Coordination Committee in which they took part. The Universality of Rome that substituted Universal Fascism, will have its influence reduced as the National Socialist star rises in the end of the 1930's, and specially during the World conflict in which Italy will no longer be a power. Therein we may see the Universal Fascism/Roman way converted in a sort of *Hispanism* such as the one defended by Franquism, without further transcendence than to try to group the countries of common culture and language, with the Universalist political aspect reduced to a very minor secondary plan. However in Italy the Universalist sectors would radically evolve to Europeistic postures during World War II. Consequently Cantillo Pellizzi will be the promoter, in 1942, of a national congress under the auspices of

---

[46] Ibid, p. 565.

the National Institute for Fascist Culture on the Idea of Europe. An identical evolution can be observed in Giuseppe Bottai that from the pages of *Crítica Fascista* maintained a constant debate on Europe being considered by the Italian scholars as the true creator and inspirer of the immediate post-War Italian Fascism's Eurofascist current. Thus, Dino Confrancesco, Italian professor that has studied this evolution, points out in his writings that *"Eurofascism was, therefore, one of the reasons for the popularity of the last and fortunate Bottaian creation."*[47]

Therefore, he outlines the Internationalist character of Universal Fascism, not only in its Universalistic guidelines but also on its doctrinal elaboration that borrowed contributions from many foreign intellectuals. Since the early days non-Italian collaborators sent their chronicles and articles to the main diffusion organs of Universal Fascism. One of the pioneers will be the British James Strachey Barnes, with his *The Universal Aspects of Fascism*. In Spain we find Ernesto Jimenez Caballero with his articles in *La Gaceta Literaria* and posterior books of essays on Italian Fascism as *Genio de España* (1932) and *La nueva Catolicidad* (1933) where he analyses Fascism as a worldwide alternative. It is specially interesting to go over the innumerable articles published in magazines as *Antieuropa* or *Ottobre*, that weren't destined to the foreign public but to the Italian one and that had *"the honor of being able to interpretate Mussolini's universal conception from the columns of our publication"*, said Gravelli in 1935 presenting the work of these intellectuals, *"young Fascist intelligentsia from all over Europe"*.[48] Characters like the Dutch Simón P. Hooms, the Spanish Ernesto Jimenez Caballero, the Germans Dr. Koppen and Hans Keller, Georg Moenius, Albert Bieler, Mommsen, Mirko Jelusich, M. Wundt, Hilckman and innumerous non-Italian names wrote there, many of whom we shall see taking part in political and intellectual European Fascist activities in the 1930's and during the conflict.

---

[47] Confrancesco, op. cit, p. 29-30.
[48] Gravelli, *Panfascismo*, op. cit., p. 11.

Revolutionary Fascism

The Lost Ideal, Europeism in the RSI, 1943-1945

As we already know the 25th of July and the following armistice of September 1943 supposed an irremediable fracture for Italy and for Fascism but did not detained Fascism's ideological evolution in its unstoppable march towards militant Europeism. From the early beginning the intellectuals and leaders of the RSI did their best to elaborate some Europeistic theoretical guidelines, not sufficient enough for the aspirations of those more radical, but even so much more developed than in the previous phase. Republican Socialism laid out as a revolutionary alternative, assumed some guidelines, among them was the certainty that Europe had been driven to the abyss as a consequence of errors from the past that should be overcome. We are not referring only to the desperate Europeism of the Waffen S.S, whose propaganda in Italy will be very effective (coined by Europeistic intellectuals such as Asvero Gravelli), nor to the propagandistic Europeism nourished by the German propaganda apparatus, but to those proposals that supposed a progress and a deepening of the social principles of the primeval Fascism, not any longer confined to the sterile debates of a few scarce intellectuals writing for cultural magazines.

The RSI included Europeism in its governance program, the first European state to do so, when of the press publishing of the *Verona Manifest* by the 15th of November 1943, its 8th point stated:

"The essential goal of the external policy must be the unity, the independence and the territorial integrity of the Fatherland in its maritime and alpine limits designated by nature, bloody sacrifice and History; borders that are threatened by the enemy due to the invasion and by the promises made to the governments that sought refuge in London. Another essential goal will consist in having recognized the necessity of indispensable vital spaces for a people of 45 million inhabitants that are located in an insufficient area to nourish them.

Furthermore, such policy shall be adopted for the setting up of a European community, federating all nations that accept the following fundamental principles:

a) *Elimination of the centennial British intrigues in our continent.*

b) *Abolition of the internal [European] Capitalist system and resolute struggle against the Plutocracies.*

c) *Valorization, on behalf of the European and Autochthonous peoples, of Africa's natural resources, with the utmost respect for those peoples, especially the Muslims, that, like in Egypt, are nationally and civically organized."*

An ambitious program… - mere rhetoric? – One that today may seem unfeasible knowing the tragic circumstances in which it was divulged. Nevertheless, as one looks closer to the crepuscular Fascism initiatives we may come to the conclusion that a true European consciousness did in fact existed in it. The Fascist leaders will do their best to further deepen this Europeistic line, as did it happened in other countries of the German orbit during those last months of the struggle, with more or less explicit declarations of intent in that way. Gino Meschiari, delegate of the Republican Fascist Party from Tuscany in the Party's National Directorate published a brochure in 1944 demanding an Europeistic orientation; the same did, by the same year, the ambassador Capasso Torre di Caprara when he published his *L'Asse e L'Europa*, all a plea in that sense.[49]

Also in 1944 the RSI's Foreign Affairs ministry came up with the idea of creating a European front of nations capable of being the USSR counterpart, to be baptized as ESRU (European Socialist Republics Union), the later had little or no real success. Fully committed to this line the Italian diplomats will try to participate in all German initiatives that concerned it, trying to influence them, but without success. In August 1944, Vittorio Mussolini wrote to Italy, from Germany, in his quality as Republican Fascist delegate for the Third Reich, a confidential report where we can grasp the frustration that these Europeists felt before the slowness of the German measures, and how convinced they were that solely an Europeistic policy could turn the conflict around:

---

[49] G. Meschiari, *Spunti di politica estera*, Venice, Casa Editrice delle Edizioni Populare, 1944.

Revolutionary Fascism

"I still believe that the German propaganda's initial mistake of not having defined the objectives of the war from the very beginning, like for instance the 'new order', and of not having officially given, until now, any update on how Europe will be structured after the victory, to be a serious one...

...nowadays one speaks of Europe, of the Napoleonic idea, of Mazzini, to create a continental front, to convince them that this is a war for a European resurgence. But it is too late and too little has been done. It would have sufficed, as I have proposed, a solemn assembly, for instance in Vienna, of the European nations leaders, of the Führer, of the Duce, of Antonescu, Laval, Pavelic, Quisling, etcetera, to reaffirm European unity".

Having embarked in his last adventure, Mussolini fully participated in the Europeistic ideal, nonetheless doubting those that wanted to absolutely surmount the 19th century nationalities. In his last grand public appearance in Milan's lyrical theatre on December the 16th 1944, one of the most important Mussolinian interventions, he shall take the time to expressly dedicate a few moments to the European question:

"With reference to this point, [referring to the Verona's Manifest 8th point] a few words about Europe are in order. I do not wish for to dwell as to enquire about Europe, where it starts and where it ends from a geographical, historical, moral and economic point of view; nor do I ask myself, today, if a unification attempt may now know a better result than the previous ones. That would take me too far. I confine myself to say that the constitution of an European community is desirable and inclusively possible, but I must declare in the most explicit way that we do not feel like as Italians because we are European, but that we feel like Europeans because we are Italians. This is not a subtle distinction but a fundamental one.

Being as it may the nation is the result of millions of families that have a physiognomy of their own and that possess a common national denominator, each nation should join the European community as a well defined entity, so to prevent that the community were to sink into Socialist Internationalism or vegetate in the generic and equivocal Cosmopolitism of a Jewish and Masonic brand".[50]

---

[50] Repr. Spampanato, op. cit., p. 688.

Erik Norling

In February, 1945, weeks away from the end, the theoretical magazine belonging to the Ministry of Economy - *Repubblica Sociale* - directed by Professor Manlio Sargenti, published a summula on the state of affairs of the European question in the RSI.[51] In an unsigned article titled "*Punto cardinali: 1) dell'unitá europea*", the different postures upholded in the Republican press on the subject were critically reviewed, helping us to have a general overview on the debate. The magazine, that represented the most radical wing of Republican Fascism, echoed the 8th point of the *Verona Manifest* and the Duce's words in Milan, explicitly rallying along with the group that is calling for a serious study of the theme: "*The problem of Europe's unity is a question that one must examine, discuss and study because it is the problem of our continent's coming tomorrow, a continent of which Italy is a part of*". This official publication recognizes, let us not forget that we are in February 1945, that defeat is near (*"all evidences point out that this will not be an agreed peace, but one imposed by the winners"*), that Italy has lost its moral authority with the armistice of the 8th of September but that this should not be an impediment for Italy to be "*an ally to Germany,…, in this final fight till the last drop of blood, its civilization, its history - carrying an idea that may have a universal valor - all of these are elements for which it must actively participate in the European construction.*"

Not by chance many of this magazine's collaborators will be found after the war in the MSI, being paladins of the Europeistic ideal in the Italian National-Revolutionary movements.[52]

---

[51] *Repubblica Sociale*, year I, n° 6, February 1945.
[52] On Europeism and NR Italian groups, see Orazio Ferrara, *El mito negato. Da Giovane Europa ad Avanguardia di Popolo. La destra erotica negli anni settanta*, Sarno, 1996.

IV
The Black Brigades: a Party at Arms

One of the most interesting chapters of the RSI's brief period was the Republican Fascist Party's (PRF) transformation into a militarized organization that encadred the most fearsome militants from Revolutionary Fascism. These units were baptized with the expressive name of Black Brigades. In a merciless war like the Italian between 1943 and 1945 both sides committed excesses, but the winners have been able to impose a sinister image of these units that were born precisely to detain the war and whose members took the bitter end of the post-war's hard repression. But they were something more; they represented the old yearning for a Party at arms, a connection between the people and the warrior class, a sort of Italian S.S but with a Revolutionary and Populist style differing from the German order that was always elitist.

The Black Brigades are born

Due to the mounting of terrorist activities the different Fascist federations had been autonomously organizing themselves in defense units composed by those black shirts that for some reason were not in the front. Early in June the idea of creating a militarized branch within the Party started to take shape, following the organizational example promoted by the Federale (governor) of Milan Vincenzo Costa that had set up a force of 1,800 men to such ends. By the end of June Mussolini approves the project. In the 25th of that month he signed the order for the constitution of the Black Brigades and by a Duce's legislative decree - the 446th dated of June 30, 1944, containing 13 articles - the birth of the so-called Black Brigades was juridically formalized, "*auxiliary corps of the black shirt action squadrons*" the decree stated, and "*civilian militia at the service of the Italian Social Republic*".

The purpose of this disposition was to transform the Republican Fascist Party into a combat unit. The decision of reorganizing the Party in a Paramilitary unit was due to the alarmingly defenseless situation of the Fascist militants and to the pessimism that reigned in the Spring-Summer of 1944. The Allies were at the gates of Rome, the Partisans were relentless in their terrorist attacks, any Fascist militant was a target and therefore they were the main victims of the GAPs. Isolated, poorly armed, the members of the PFR were ideal targets for some terrorist groups that avoided confrontation with military units but cowardly slaughtered any individual when found isolated and defenseless, following a strategy of terror ordered by the chiefs of staff of Moscow and Washington. The birth of the Black Brigades intended to remediate this distressing situation - by promoting self-defense in all of the Fascist sections - thus maintaining the structure of a party that risked disbandment as well as to create a paramilitary structure capable of opposing the terrorists using the same weapons.

A month later, July 25, the general secretary of the PFR, Alessandro Pavolini, speaking from Radio Turin, detailed the structure and functions of the Black Brigades (BN in the military nomenclature of the RSI) thus automatically incorporating in the Brigades all the members of the PFR over 18 and under 60 years of age that didn't belong to any military formation. The Party's directorate was therefore transformed in a sort of paramilitary corps chief of staff, not in a parallel police thought, given that its functions were clearly delimited from the start. The Black Brigades weren't supposed to play a role in the maintaining of public order, but to repress the terrorist groups, a boundary that was difficult to delimitate. For this purpose the minister of the Interior was obliged to telegraph to the provincial leaders in the 26th of August 1944, *"I say yet again that by Mussolini's order any police action by the Brigades stands forbidden"*. Each Brigade would carry the name of a martyr of the Republican Fascist cause and it would be permitted for any PFR militant serving in a military unit to apply for a transfer to the Black Brigades in order to be closer to his family.

The objectives pursued by Pavolini were not solely of self-defense, as one could have thought at first, they went much beyond that. The Revolutionary origins [of Fascism] and its dream of a popular revolution were not foreigners to the maximal leader of the PFR when he announced the creation of the BB. Himself a son of this earliest hour Revolutionary Fascism - he had marched on Rome in 1922 – known as an essayist, from a distinguished family of intellectuals, Florentine Fascism was his fief, also the cradle of so many of the Party leaders. In October, 1939, he was

Revolutionary Fascism

appointed minister of Popular Culture, in what intended to be the equivalent to Dr. Goebbels' ministry in Germany. In February, 1943, he abandoned the ministry to direct the daily *Il Messagero*, yet again in the same year he had no doubts whatsoever as to take Mussolini's side, this one ordered him to reconstruct the Party. Therefore he will turn out to be a key character in the RSI.

The BB, in the words of Pavolini, should symbolize fidelity, "*the fidelity of those men that haven't betrayed, that haven't hesitated, having given their life to one Ideal and to a Leader.*" Words that inexorably remind us of the SS motto: "*My honor is loyalty*".

Organization

The chain of command of the Black Brigades was simple, each one was autonomous, but with a sole command always subordinated to the Party alone, never to the German authorities or to the Graziani's Armed Forces. At the head of the Brigades was, for that reason, the general secretary of the PFR, Alessandro Pavolini, acting as a divisional general. Pavolini will be the central piece in Republican Fascism and the main promoter of the Brigades creation against Graziani's opinion that would have preferred a traditional style army without interferences from autonomous unit's independent from the military chain of command. The Fascist militants, leaded by their local party officers, were under military discipline and laws.

In each city a brigade was set up to assure its security, the remaining provincial effectives were organized into another one, a mobile brigade, in order to patrol the region, travelling around it. Pavolini's deputy chief, coordinator of all of the Brigades, was Puccio Pucci. The colonel Giovanni Battista Riggio took over the Brigades' general staff (substituted in October 30, 1944, by general Eduardo Facdouelle), that was organized to resemble a division's general staff, with its inspections, commissary, court-martial, chaplains, etc. By November, 1944, a war court-martial was constituted exclusively for the BB. This was done in order to further detach them from the Armed Forces.

As Party militias, not explicitly constituted as military units, they had no ranks; they used the ones from the Party, nevertheless the company and battalion leaders (on this subject the Brigades followed military nomenclature) received military denominations: lieutenant, captain, commander. The [brigades] enlisted Black Shirt was called "*Squadrista*" accordingly to the vocabulary inaugurated during the turmoil years that preceded the taking of power in 1922. This differentiated him from the non-combatant [in the Black Brigades] party member. The uniform, according to regulations, was constituted by a black shirt or jersey, a military cap, black, with a skull and crossed bones upfront, military trousers and the Party badge, the Fascio Littorio, in red. In the collar some formations wore their own kind of badges. In the winter they would use army jackets. The unit leaders were also distinguishable by the fact that they carried a white shoulder cord on their right side. Nevertheless the BB's were militias after all and that gave way to the proliferation of badges, insignia, uniforms and other attires.

It is interesting to point out that the female militants could also play their part in Fascism's defense. The women's role in Fascism was always a prominent and appreciated one, so their support would not fail in these hard times either. To each brigade was attached a feminine auxiliary corps, Servizio Ausiliario Femmenile, to whom was assigned intendancy missions, administration and other auxiliary services while the men were in the front line. Many of them were Fascists' daughters and wives that shared those ideals. They will suffer in their own flesh the terrorist actions and in the post-war they will be crucial to the preservation of the ideal that got them to put on the black shirt when many of their husbands and fathers had already fallen in the struggle.

Revolutionary Fascism

An Eye for an Eye

The reputation of the Black Brigades will build up as the civil war mounts. It is a combat without mercy and without quarrel. Both sides go to extreme lengths in their intention of exterminating the opponent. Talion Law is the rule. It doesn't go unnoticed by anyone that this terrible reaction-counter reaction, provoked by the Communists and Socialists, bore its fruits when the Fascists decided to arm and defend themselves. The Fascist ideology's kind words and its desire of appeasement were pushed into the background. We must acknowledge that the Black Brigades were part of that terrible spiral of hate and violence in which they were engulfed preventing them of having the time to reflect.

In some occasions the Brigades acted in cooperation with the military authorities, in fact all of the Squadristi were combatants (no one considered necessary a special training for these units), they were soon to have many casualties. Pavolini himself took part in several anti-Partisan actions, being wounded in the 12th of August 1944, when leading an anti-Partisan patrol. That no one was trying to dodge the front line is shown by the fact that in the same ambush both the vicefederale (sub governor) of Turin as the Brescia's federal commissar were seriously injured. Overall about 30,000 Fascist militants will be encadred in the 59 Black Brigades that were formed. A report from general Facdouelle, dated from April 1945, states: *"the Black Brigades, as of today, consist of 29,000 men at arms. Eleven Brigade commanders have fallen in combat as well as 47 officers, 1,641 Squadristi and nine feminine auxiliary."* The high number of fallen Brigade Leaders, 11 no less, shows that practically one in each five Brigades lost at least one of its commanders during those bloody months of 1944-45. Each province and major city will have its own brigade. The main ones are, from Milan, the "Aldo Resega", Turin's "Ather Cappelli", from Aosta the "Emilio Picot", Novara's "Augusto Cristina", etc.

Without a doubt the most famous will be the Milanese "Aldo Resega". Founded in the June, 30, 1934 it consisted of more than 4,000 armed Squadristi, in two battalions, having had at least 600 casualties. The first battalion was assigned to the city of Milan, the 2ⁿᵈ one to the province, the name of the Brigade corresponded to the first Republican Fascist federale murdered the 8ᵗʰ of December, 1943, in Milan, Aldo Resega, shot down by a Communist group. The Brigade commander will be the city's Fascist federale Vincenzo Costa. Not to be mistaken with the notorious Autonomous Legion Ettore Mutti[53] that acted independently from the Black Brigades.

Sunset of the Gods

The last heroic acts of Italian Fascism were protagonized by these fighters in Black shirt. In the afternoon of the 25ᵗʰ of April 1945, when the German capitulation in Italy is known for a fact, the largest part[54] of the "Aldo Resega's" mobile battalion departs to the north, towards Ivrea. Meanwhile, the city battalion entrenches itself in the Milanese headquarters of the PFR willing to resist. Those headquarters were situated in the San Sepolcro Piazza, where Fascism was founded in 1919. However, they received instructions from their commander to join a column of several Black Brigades that are retreating towards Como.

The 26ᵗʰ of April, at dawn, a column composed by the "Aldo Resega" Brigade together with the Black Brigades "Tognu", Turchetti", "Azzara", "Fachini", "Capanni", "Cavazzoni", "Tevere" and "Ricciarelli", departs from Milan. They are accompanied by the men of the Autonomous Legion Mutti and of the Republican National Guard as well.

Until they reached Mornasco the itinerary had been covered without incident, exiting the village the column is attacked by British fighter aircrafts. In a matter of seconds, an ammunition truck explodes killing two Squadristi and seriously wounding a female auxiliary. Nevertheless the Fascist machine guns are able to bring down a British aircraft. Finally they arrive to Como where they await orders to proceed with their march to the

---

[53] Editor's note: this one included a battalion also named after Aldo Resega.

[54] The Squadristi from its 3ʳᵈ company stationed at the San Damiano's Macra prison were all massacred.

Revolutionary Fascism

Valtellina - the stronghold where it was thinkable to resist and to defend the Duce - but these do not arrive. The ones they receive in the morning of the 27th are confuse. They carry on with their march but are surrounded by Partisans in Cernobbio, where they are forced to surrender being assassinated and executed by the dozens.

The fortune of the remaining members of the Black Brigades was equally tragic. The majority of the "Aldo Resega's" mobile battalion that - as we already saw – hadn't accompanied the main column was also assailed by the Communists on the 25th of April but they manage to repel the attacks with the aid of an Alpine Hunters unit. On the afternoon of the 27th the unit reaches Savigliano where it rests and regroups, scattered Fascist units also join them to seek refuge. The open season for Fascists was unleashed far and wide. They had been joined by the men of the Black Brigades of Cuneo and Savigliano as well as by Alpine Hunters commanded by a colonel. When they reach their objective, Ivrea, between Turin and Como, no one but the Partisans is expecting them. Nevertheless they will resist their attacks until the arrival of the American troops in the 5th of May, to whom they surrender with military honors, thus avoiding execution at the hands of the communists.

The Squadristi far outposts in rural villages and settlements progressively surrender to the Partisans but are immediately annihilated without mercy or due process. With the end of the war comes the worst part of this terrible repression. The Communists slaughter families and members of the BBs (their yesteryear's worst enemies) and thousands of them will be vilely murdered during the bloody "expurgation" of 1945-46. Pavolini himself will be assassinated, such as almost all of the Brigade leaders, by Communist Partisans. Some authors have considered that the BBs suffered casualties up to approximately 60% in combat (including the post-War repression).

The bloody post-War shall suscitate the early appearance of neo-Fascist groups as the memory of the fallen must be respected and their names rehabilitated. A consequence not foresaw by Communists and Socialists when they unleashed civil war and that decisively helped, as we already now, to the creation of a neo-Fascist mass movement. The veterans converged into associations whose goal was to contrast the horrible image of the BBs in the public opinion. Hence was born, for example, the Associazione D'Arma Fiammanere of Milan, part of the Unione Nazionale Combattenti Della RSI[55]. Its activities have been numerous and diversified, among them the edition, for decades now, of a magazine, "La Legione", dedicated to the BBs and that constitutes a considerable source of information for historians.

---

[55] National Union of Veterans of the RSI, editor's note.

Revolutionary Fascism

V
The "Socialisers" of Italian Fascism (1922-1945)

A major intellectual debate broke out in Italy when of the publication by the Bologna's well known publishing house Il Mulino, of the extensive and documented essay by Giuseppe Parlato, *Fascismo di Sinistra. Storia de un progetto mancato*[56] [*Leftwing Fascism. History of a failed project*]. The subjacent thesis that has scandalized numerous sectors of the *politically correct* Italian Leftwing *intelligentsia* is that Fascism may have had a large Leftwing component, much larger than it was perceived until now, thus breaking away with one of the most divulged myths that defined it as being a *Far Right* doctrine. This discussion, however, is not new; already at the beginning of the 1990's, when the first serious works on the subject were published, one could assert how mistaken had been Fascism's approach until then.

Fascism, Left-Winger?

It is no destiny's irony that Nicola Bombacci - founder of Italian Communism – was to be shot down together with other Fascist hierarchs in April 1945. Nor that in the last months of Fascism, in the so called Italian Social Republic (RSI), were to be applied politics and principles that many considered extremely leftist, a moment in which, furthermore, the language and the aesthetics were proletarized. The *Verona Manifest*, laws such as the one of 1944 on Socialization, the workers councils, the companies' co-management, the Socialist-Republican state ideation, made of the *last Mussolini* and of his Republican Fascism a permanent paradox. How to accommodate the Marxist historian's propaganda together with the adamant reality of the facts? In what way could this historic period be encadred without recognizing its singularity? How to legitimate an Antifascist resistance that was precisely built upon the myth of having

---

[56] Expert in Syndicalist history at the Fascist stage, he authored numerous works on the subject: *La politica sociale e sindicale 1930-1938*, in *Annali della Economia Italiana*, coordinated by G. Rasi, Milan, 1983, Vol. VIII, 1, pp. 293 and next; *Il syndicalism fascista. Dalla grande crisi alla caduta del regime (1930-1943)*, Rome, 1988.

fought against the enemies of the Italian worker? Quite simply, a curtain of Silence was drawn, by-passed by a handful of nostalgic that, by the skin of their teeth, have gone to great lengths to preserve the sources, a task that we must qualify as extraordinary and that History - in caps - someday will have to thank generously. The taboos have lingered after six decades, but nowadays Italian historians have settled to re-examine the past with an unused interest[57].

Fascist Socialism is rooted in the very tradition of Fascism as a revolutionary movement, being that Socialism and Revolutionary Syndicalism decisively contributed to its foundation. This apparent paradox may surprise at first, being Fascism a complex phenomenon as it is, but by other hand it explains it and, indeed, facilitates its interpretation.

In the beginning, the Mussolinian regime was perceived as a Socialist reaction, only with the International Communist instructions of strict opposition to Fascism (second half of the 1930's), will the equation Fascism = Far Right take shape setting a "standard". Thus, we can read in a propaganda bulletin from a Communist inclined publisher, and therefore unsuspicious of Fascist tendencies, printed in 1933 in Valencia, that "*Fascism as a... intimate... relation with the ideas of Sorel*", simultaneously he recognizes that many of the former Italian Socialist leaders were now on the Fascist side.[58] Identical reflection made, in those years, a then young Communist that wrote on Fascism, a political doctrine, in which he saw, more than a mere enemy of Communism, a serious competitor in the conquest of the state and of the Proletarian masses. Montero Díaz, that afterwards will turn out to be a Fascist doctrinator in Spain, wrote quoting another Communist/Fascist, Curzio Malaparte, that "*the tactic followed by Mussolini to seize the state could not have been conceived by no other than a Marxist. We must not ever forget that Mussolini's education is a Marxist one*"[59].

---

[57] As claims the Italian Fascism historian's *Summo Pater*, Renzo de Felice, considered to be the most notorious authority on this period. His revisionist thesis caused him more than one problem even though he is of Hebrew origin and a former member of the Communist Party. On the debate about the convenience of studying the RSI see *Rojo y Negro*, Barcelona, Ariel, 1996.

[58] Gaetan Pirou, *Georges Sorel (1847-1922)*, p. 34-35.

[59] Santiago Montero Díaz, *Fascismo*, Cuadernos de Cultura, Valencia, 1932, p.25.

Revolutionary Fascism

From the San Sepolcro Piazza to the Verona congress

In 1989 Luca Leonello Rimbotti published his revealing study *Il fascismo di Sinistra. Da Piazza San Sepolcro al congresso di Verona.*[60] The polemic was unleashed. Several were the historians that polemized about it, opening by inertia, an historigraphic debate on the role of Fascism and its condition in the Italian society, its outcome was, we may say with a degree of certainty, the beginning of the demystification of a good part of the negative prejudices that were held against this historical period. In the same year, in France, got published *The birth of Fascist ideology*[61], a fundamental study, coordinated by the Israeli professor Zeev Sternhell. In it, Sternhell and his team, until then almost exclusively dedicated to the French origins of Fascism, abounded in the revolutionary origins of early Fascism and analyzed in detail the gestation of a Revolutionary Syndicalism, markedly Socialist, that inspired by the Revolutionary theorists from the late 19th and early 20th centuries, will be the germen of which Fascism will be born.

We should bear in mind that the first proposals, the ones that were proclaimed in the foundational act of the Combat Fascii (Milan, 1919), had an enormous Revolutionary accent from which none would predict the Ventennio's future connivance with the traditional powers (Church, Finance, Reactionary Agrarianism…): Republicanism, universal suffrage, abolition of nobility titles, dissolution of private financial entities, uphold of labor-value superiority weighed against capital-valor, Agrarian reform, international solidarity against imperialism. That did not stop Fascism of waving the *Red peril* flag to attract the most sensitive anti-Bolshevik sectors of Italian society. There was no contradiction whatsoever in this discourse, even though the Duce's former companions would catalogue him as a "traitor", being that he saw Fascism as an *overcome*, a *Third Way*, both of the Right as of the Left, still he would never renegate his Socialist origins, he was nevertheless utterly convinced that he had overcame them. On the subject, Mussolini even wrote that *"in the great river of Fascism thou shall find the currents that spring from Sorel, from Lagardelle's Movement Socialiste, from Péguy, and from the Italian Syndicalists cohort."*[62]

---

[60] Rome, Settimo Sigillo, 1989.
[61] Princeton University Press, 1995.
[62] Vallecchi, Florence, 1937, p. 26.

Erik Norling

In 1922 Mussolini seized power and immediately started a series of reforms that aroused admiration around the world. To do that, however, he had to make a pact with the traditional powers and withdraw (or freeze) some of his initial proposals. The most revolutionary sectors of the Party concentrated in the Unions, raised their voices in protest in more than one occasion. The *intransigents*, as were called the Fascists that demanded Mussolini to put into practice the pending revolution (a vocabulary that, curiously, would be assumed in Spain by the Falangists *discontented* with the Franquist regime), were practically defenestrated or *incorporated* (again the similarities with Spain is evident) into the Fascist state before the end of the 1920's.[63]

Fascism, Communism

Fascism's last months in power, the Italian Social Republic (RSI), were - as we already mentioned - extremely intense and passionate. They witnessed the rebirth of the Fascist wing baptized as Leftist, which, in reality, was the main loser in 1945. The civil war was directed against it, initiated by the Communists to end the influence that these resolute Fascist Proletarian leaders could exercise on the workers. The secretary general of the Republican Fascist Party, Alessandro Pavolini, came from the Florentine nucleus, one that had distinguished itself for its contribution, during the Ventennio, of Syndicalist and Socialization theorists to Fascism.[64] Shortly after the war, many of these Leftwing Fascists were - when the bloody repression came to an end - received with open arms by the Communists, as they needed capable leaders to encadre and organize the PCI's Unions. Professor Pietro Neglie, from the Trieste University, studied in detail this transfer of Fascist Syndicalist militants to the Communist Unions in *Fratelli in camicia nera. Comunisti e fascisti dal corporativismi alia CGIL (1928-1948)*[65], where one concludes that the so-called transfer was the logical consequence of some militant guidelines gestated by Fascism itself,

---

[63] Pietro Neglie, *Confronto: Il fascismo di sinistra*, public debate with Marco Tarchi in the 29th of October, 1998, in Boulogne, organized by the town council's culture office, reproduced in *Diorama Letterario*, June 2000, Florence, p. 12.

[64] In the same conferences where Neglie and Tarchi debated there was also a presentation by Alessandro Soldani, *Alessandro Pavolini: il partito fascista republicano, la sinistra fascista al potere*.

[65] Bologna, Il Mulino, 1996.

Revolutionary Fascism

resolutely emerging in the Social Republic, but whose direct priors must be sought in the mid 1920's.

We may find an identical contribution to the history of the so considered defeated Social Republic survivors' Leftist wing in the detailed study of Paolo Buchignani, *Fascisti rossi. Da Salò al PCI. La storia consociate di una migrazione política 1943-53*.[66] In it are revealed the connections and intents to attract the ex-Republicans, as they were called, by a PCI sector using Stanis Ruinas as a connecting thread. Ruinas was a veteran Fascist leader that will accompany Mussolini during the Ventennio and the Social Republic - in some occasions subjected to disciplinary sanctions, in others reconciled with the Fascist regime - that in such a later date as February, 1945, kept on publishing Revolutionary proclamations. Anti-Americanism, Europeism, anti-Zionism and Socialism were arguments that drove him closer to the PCI than to the Rightwing. Orbiting around this singular character, a well nourished group of Mussolinian followers will find their way to the Left through Communism[67].

Another noteworthy group of Fascist militants, whose anti-Communism prevented them from embracing the Leftist side although they were closer to it than to the Rightist one converged, having founded right in the middle of the post-War era the *Movimiento Sociale Italiano*. This party will play a very relevant role in Italian politics. The MSI's Syndicalist section got to encadre more than a million of Italian workers in its better years during the 1970's. This movement, that grouped numerous tendencies, from Rightwing Monarchists to National-Popular Revolutionaries, was *per se* distinguishable by its maintaining for propaganda purposes the *last of Mussolini's* most revolutionary arguments, always claiming to be his *spiritual heirs* (and, in practice, also *material* ones, for it was not in vain that many of its first leaders had been also leaders of the Republican Fascist

---

[66] Mondadori, Milan, 1998. Likewise author of an interesting and no less pioneer essay on the figure of the frustrated Fascist leader Marcello Galian, *La bataglia antiborghese di un fascista anarchico*, Rome, Bonacci Editore, 1988.

[67] Stanis Ruinas, was really named Giovanni Antonio de Rosas, from Sardinia (1899-1984). Journalist by profession and a famous writer in the 1930's, he will serve in Spain as a war correspondent with the Italian Volunteer Corps during the Spanish Civil War. "For the glory of Rome and for the triumph of Falangist Spain", wrote he in the dedication of the book he wrote in 1939 upon his return, *Vecchi e nuova Spagna*, Milan, Garzanti Editore, 1940.

Party).⁶⁸ Secessionists from the MSI along with groups born of its radiance or orbit shall converge in the 1960-70's into the National-Communism rim. Well known are the connections of many National-Revolutionary group leaders from that period onwards shall reemerge encadred in the Italian Leftwing, including in Radical Leftist groups, such as the Red Brigades⁶⁹.

Epilogue

The debate's vitality in Italy, even though in the rest of the continent it may be smothered by the nowadays asphyxiating ideological lid of "political correctness", outlines a reality that cannot be dodged: that the true history of Fascism is still being written, a situation that, for obvious reasons, shall only be resolved when the prejudices and myths of the Antifascist propaganda have definitively evaporated. Certainly, the Fascist phenomenon, the *great revolution of ideas* as it was qualified by its contemporary's coreligionists, was a phenomenon as broad as complex. The simplification and generalization made by Marxism-Leninism (also adopted for convenience and/or by cowardice by the Rightwing authors that *went along with it*) neither helped, nor help, or will ever help its comprehension. Only if one's starting point is that Fascism was an *open cosmos*, that enclosed all of the society's layers, where practically all citizens could be fitted in, only then, a significant step will be made towards to an accomplished comprehension of the Fascist phenomenon. *Good deeds or perversions* aside.

---

⁶⁸ For a vindication of this principles from the *misino*'s [nickname of the members of the MSI] side, see Giano Accame, *Il fascismo inmenso e rosso*, Rome, Settimo Sigillo, 1990; Enrico Landolfi, *Ciao, rossa Salò. Il crepúsculo libertario e socializzatore di Mussolini ultimo*, Rome, Edizioni delloleandro, 1996.

⁶⁹ For an excellent work on the subject, see Orazio Ferrara, *Il mito begato da giovanne Europa ad Avanguardia di popolo. La destra eretica negli anni settanta*, Sarno, 1996. For the Spanish language readers, see Anonymous, *De Joven Europa a las Brigadas Rojas. Anti-Americanism y lògica de la tarea Revolucionario*, Alternativa Europea, 1996.

Appendage

I
Separation from the Socialist Italian Party

(Speech pronounced by Mussolini in the 25th of November, 1914, before the Milan's Socialist Assembly, held in the People's Theatre, that decided his expulsion from the Socialist Party.)

My fortune it is cast, and it seems that you would like to give a certain atmosphere of solemnity to the act of my elimination.

Some voices: Forte! Forte![70] *(The speaker, before such an imperious insistence, nervously knocks in the table with a glass).*

You are more severe than the Bourgeois judges, who always enable the possibility for a broader and thorough defense, even after the condemnatory sentence has been pronounced, conceding ten days for a just appeal. Well then, if the matter is already settled, if you corroborate your will to declare me unworthy of standing among you...

- Yes, yes! - Cry out at a same voice the most exalted.

Expel me if you will; but I have the right to demand an accusation in due form. In this assembly the prosecution has not yet put forward neither the political question nor the moral one, in fact I am being beheaded due to an order of the day that doesn't say anything at all. On it, what was expected was to be categorically said: "you are unworthy of being among us for that or those motives", and then I would have accepted my faith. However, nothing of the sort has been said to me, and many of you, not to say all, will leave with remorse in your conscience.

Loud voices: - No! No!

As for the moral question, I say once more that I am ready to submit to a commission -whatever one- that enquires about it and presents its report.

In what concerns the matter of discipline, I say that this one has not been put forward, or anything of the sort, because there are real and accurate precedents that, however, I shall not invocate, because I'm sure of myself, having a clean conscience. You believe that you have lost me, however I say on to you that you are wrong. You hate me because you still

---

[70] Translator's note: Italian expression of strong disagreement, resembling a hiss.

love me, because... (*Once more the speaker is interrupted by both applause and hisses*).

But, you shall not lose me; twelve years of my life dedicated to the party, are, or should be, guaranty enough of my Socialist faith. Socialism is something that has its roots in blood itself. That which separates us today, is a question of no little value, it is a transcendental issue that divides the whole of Socialism. Amilcare Cipriani, in whose name we have led a remarkable struggle in the Sixth Electoral College (do you remember that hard-fought dispute?) Amilcare Cipriani can no longer be your candidate, because he has declared both by word and in writing that if not by his 75 years, he would already be in the trenches fighting against the European militarist reaction that suffocates the Revolution. Time will tell, and then one should see clearly who was wrong and who was right in this formidable matter that had never before been faced by Socialism, simply because also never before in the history of mankind had this one faced such a conflict, in which millions of Proletarians fight each other. Such a war as the present one does not break every day, it has some resemblance with the Napoleonic epopee. Waterloo was in 1814; we shall see if in 1914 another principle is to be overthrown, another throne to fall into pieces, if another crown is to be shattered; perhaps we can rescue freedom, initiating a new era in the world's history ... (*applauses*) specially in the history of the Proletariat, who, in all of the critical hours has seen me standing my ground, here, in this very place, and also in the streets.

But I also tell you that from now on I will pardon no one, I will show no mercy to those which in this tragic hour will not speak out by fear of hiss or cries of disapproval.

(*Applauses*).

There will be no pardon, no mercy, to all the reticent, to the hypocrites, to the cowards! As to me, you shall find me always at your side. Do not believe that the Bourgeoisie sees with enthusiasm our interventionist attitude; by the contrary, it murmurs, it accuses us of being venturesome and trembles with the thought that the Proletariat, provisioned with bayonets, may use them for other ends.

(*Some applaud; others cry out: No! No!*)

Do not believe, even for a moment, that by striping me of my membership card you do the same to my Socialist believes, nor that you would restrain me of continuing to work in favor of Socialism and of the Revolution. (*Applauses*).

II
Fascism's foundational program
(February 23rd, 1919)

(Delivered by Mussolini in the hall of the Industrial Alliance Circle in the Piazza of San Sepolcro, Milan)

More than a hundred of followers and sympathizers were present when Mussolini presented his program that has always been considered as tainted with strong *Leftwing* connotations. The fundamental points were:

1) To convene a National Constituency Assembly.

2) Proclamation of the Italian Republic. Decentralization and autonomies. Popular sovereignty carried out by universal suffrage and equality of rights for citizens of both sexes. Routing out of the irresponsible burocracy and reorganization of the state's administration starting from scratch.

3) Abolition of the Senate and of the political police; creation of a Citizen's Guard.

4) Abolition of all caste titles, maintaining only the ones of honor and nobleness of talent and those derived from the honorability of work.

5) Abolition of the conscript military service, general disarmament and prohibition of manufacturing any bellicose artifacts in the country.

6) Freedom of thought and conscience, of religion, of association, press, propaganda, collective and individual agitation…

7) (…)

8) (…)

9) Dissolution of all anonymous societies and financial industries, suppression of all kinds of speculation originating from the banks and stock markets.

10) Survey and reduction of individual fortunes. Confiscation of non-productive revenues. Payment of the former state debt by those considered wealthy.

11) Interdiction of child labor under 16. Legally prescribed work journey of eight daily hours. Banishment of parasites not useful to society.

12) Direct participation of the useful citizens in every component of labor. Land for the peasants. The industries, transportation and public services will be administrated by unions of technicians and workers. Elimination of every sort of personal speculation.

13) Abolition of the secret diplomacy.

14) International politic inspired in the people's solidarity.

III
Program of the Italian Combat Fasci

Italians!

Behold the national program of a sanely Italian movement.

Revolutionary, for it is anti-dogmatic and anti-demagogic; powerfully innovator, for it is striped of any sort of preconceptions. We consider revolutionary war as the more important matter, above everyone and everything else.

All the other problems: burocracy, administration, law, schools, colonies, etc., we will address them when we have created the ruling class.

That's why we want:

Regarding the political program

a) Universal suffrage with voting by Regionalist scrutiny and proportional representation, voting rights and equality for women.

b) Lowering of the age admission limit to 18 years of age for the voters and 25 for the MPs.

c) Abolition of the Senate.

d) Summoning by a three year period, of a National Assembly that will have as a main task to establish the form of the state's constitution.

e) Setting up of work technical national counsels, in industry, in transportation, in social hygiene, in communications, etc., elected by the professional or trade collectivities, with legislative powers and the right to elect a general counsel to the legislative powers and the right to elect a general commissar empowered as a minister.

Regarding the social problem

We want:

a) Swift promulgation of a law that enforces the legal eight hours daily work journey for all of the workers.

b) Minimum wages.

c) Participation of the worker's representatives in the industry's technical management.

d) Granting to the Proletarian organizations (in so far that these may be worthy of it moral and materially) the management of industries or public services.

e) Swift and complete organization of the railroad workers and of all industries and transportations.

f) A necessary modification of the bill of law on impairment and old age insurances policies for to lower the age admittance limit from 65 to 55 years.

Regarding the military problem

We want:

a) The setting up of a national militia, with brief periods of instruction and an exclusively defensive goal.

b) Nationalization of all armament and explosives industries.

c) A national foreign policy able to emphasize the Italian Nation's valor before the world, in civilization's pacific competitions.

Regarding the financial problem

We want:

a) An extraordinary heavy taxation, with a progressive character, on capital, that will represent an authentic partial expropriation of all wealth.

b) Seizure of all assets of the religious congregations and suppression of all the ecclesiastic Episcopal revenues, in what constitutes an enormous deficit for the nation and a privilege for a minority.

c) Revision of all contracts made by the war ministers and seizure of 85% of all war profits.[71]

---

[71] In the Fasci Italiani di Combattimento (Italian Combat Fasci) is the seed of what later will become the Fascist National Party. The program here reproduced was published by the first time in *Il Popolo d'Italia* in June 6, 1919, newspaper founded and directed by Benito Mussolini.

Revolutionary Fascism

IV
Benito Mussolini's speech to the Italian people (18th of September, 1943)

Blackshirts! Italians!

After a prolonged silence you once again hear my voice. I'm sure that you will recognize it. It is the same voice that so many times has summoned you in the difficult hours and that with you has celebrated the Fatherland's most beautiful journeys.

For some days now I have hesitated to once again present me before thee. I needed to regain contact with the outside world, after a period of moral isolation.

The radio is not suitable for long speeches. As such I will not invest much time in previous events, but will start by referring to those of 25th of July.

It was the most incredible vicissitude of my life, already so rich in adventures. My conversation with the king lasted for little more than twenty minutes. All agreement was by then already impossible, given that the king had already made up his mind. The crisis unleash was imminent. It is not uncommon both in times of peace as of war that a certain minister may be exonerated or a given general sacked; But it is a unique fact in history that a man as the one who addresses you today, having served his king with absolute, I stress it once again, with absolute fidelity for more than twenty years, were to be arrested in the very own royal's residence stairs, forced into an ambulance with the pretext of saving him of an alleged plot, and then taken at mad velocity from a Carabinieri's barrack to another. Already when they transferred me to Ponza I was taken by a sudden suspicion, to be converted in certainty when from there I was taken to La Magdalena Island and from it to the Gran Sasso, that among the adopted projects I was to be handed over to the enemy. Although without communication with the exterior world I had, however, the firm inner feeling that the Führer cared for my person more as a brother than as a comrade. The word fidelity has a profound sense, or better said an eternal sense in the German's soul, a sense that is reflected, both in general and in the particular, in their spiritual world. I was sure that I would receive a proof of it. Taking notice of the conditions of the armistice I hadn't the slightest doubt about the meaning of article 12. A high rank civil servant told me that I was a hostage. In the night from the 11th to the 12th of September, however, I made known that I would not fall alive in the enemy's hands.

In the diaphanous mountain air it floated an ambience of expectation. At 2 pm I saw the first parachutist coming down, followed by the rest, willing to vanquish any sort of resistance. The people that had me under their custody realized it and didn't open fire. All of this has taken place in a few minutes. The rescue, all the action in general, constitutes an example of the German organization and decision that will go down in History, and a fact that time shall convert into a legend. This ends the chapter that one could name my personal drama, and that is but an insignificancy when compared with the horrible tragedy in which the democratic government has engulfed the Italian people in the 25th of July.

Some Fascists' incredible optimism had it as inadmissible that the government were to hold such catastrophic projects against the party, the regime and the nation itself. However the measures dictated immediately after July the 25th already outlined a program whose goals were to destroy twenty years of work, erasing twenty years of glory for to wipe out the memory of an empire's creation and of a statute never before achieved by the Fatherland. Today, before the ruins of war, that continues, some seek, desperately, to reach a compromise, quibbling and trying to find attenuating excuses for all matters concerning their responsibility, enduring in error. The ones that nowadays attack the party are the same self-indulgent beings that already in the beginning of our Movement sought to sabotage the Social advancement and to diminish our national and imperial achievements. Meanwhile, as for us, we fully assume our responsibility, let us now put to proof the one of others, starting by the first of them all.

The king, that has already been unmasked, but that against the desire of the majority of the Italians, has not abdicated, has a direct responsibility. He has represented his dynasty in every period and episode of the war, declared by him, turning out to be the center of defeatism and of anti-German propaganda. He, the most cautious of all, although sometimes he would not be so, made his all of the enemy's speculations, in the meantime his heir assumed the command of the southern army without ever showing himself in the battlefield. I am convinced that it was the House of Savoy, together with its accomplice Badoglio, a few coward generals and some traitors from the Fascist Party ranks, that firstly prepared, to its last details, and afterwards undertook, the coup d'état. There can be no doubt that immediately after my detention Badoglio received plenipotentiary powers

Revolutionary Fascism

to set up negotiations seeking an armistice, negotiations that had already been initiated before my arrest, between the House of Savoy and England. Therefore, the king has betrayed Germany in a most regrettable way, inclusively going to such length as to deny, after the armistice had been signed, that such negotiations had existed. The dynasty itself, the one I had saved from crumbling twenty years ago, has been the one that has created, according to the ancient statute of 1848, a new government and a new freedom under the sign of a state of war and of the bayonets. In what concerns the terms of the armistice, that should be generous ones, they are instead the hardest one can imagine. Nothing about these terms, not even my foreseen handing over to the enemy, had merit the king's objection. Exclusively by the sole care of his crown he has launched Italy into chaos, shame and misery. In all continents, from the Far East to America, the felonies of the House of Savoy are well known. Not even our enemies that coerced us into this shameful capitulation hide the contempt they feel for us. Since the moment this shame has befallen us, it may happen that an Italian, inclusively in its private matters, becomes suspicious in the eyes of others. If this situation were to affect solely the group of the authentically responsible, one could accept it; but one must convey that the consequences of this shame strike all Italians, from the first to the last.

After losing our honor, we have also lost the countries that we have occupied on this war: the possessions in the Adriatic, the Jonick and in the Aegean Sea, in Southern France and in the Balkans. The army, humiliated and left in the lurch, has disbanded, being disarmed by its own allies, before the mockery of the civil population.

This humiliation had to be endured both by soldiers and officers that in so many battlefields, side by side with their German allies, had fought so bravely.

Also in the Russian and African cemeteries, where so many heroes lay, and in other battlefields were do Italians and Germans rest together, after their last stand, this very same shame has been felt. The Italian Royal Navy, created during this last flourishing twenty years, has surrendered to the enemy in Malta. In that stronghold of British imperialism in the Mediterranean that constantly threatens the Italian vital interests. These are the responsibilities exposed also by the Führer in his last speech and that underline Badoglio's treason, who inclusively after the capitulation allowed the bombardment of small and large cities of Italy's south and center with the objective of misleading the Germans. Fascism hasn't betrayed the Monarchy; it was the last that all by itself has managed such that no one trusts in it anymore. Nevertheless, the unity of the Italian people has not gone under. If the Monarchy is not able to fulfill its historical role, it loses its purpose. By other hand, the fundamental Italian tendencies were always more Republican then Monarchist until the advent of Italy's unification era. It was Mazzini's Republican Movement that fought the Italian Monarchies, mostly foreigners.

The new state, that we aim to lay the foundations of, will be National and social in the broader sense; it will be a Fascist state with the same orientation that it had in its early stage.

Being convinced that our movement will be irresistible, we formulate the following demands:

1) Resuming of the struggle side by side with Germany, Japan and the remaining allies. Only blood can erase such a dishonorable page in our Fatherland's History.

2) Immediate reconstruction of the army that will regroup itself around a core constituted by the Militia. Only the one that bears arms and that fights for his creed may win.

3) Elimination of the traitors, particularly those that in July 25, at 9:30 pm, have recognized the new government, thus joining the enemy ranks.

4) Elimination of the Plutocracy and establishment of a Social basis upon which to build the state, sustained by the labor of its citizens.

Blackshirts; faithful supporters from the whole of Italy! Once again I call upon thee to labor and to arms. The enemy's joy due to Italy's capitulation does not mean that they already have victory at hand. Our allies, Germany and Japan, will continue to fight until final victory, without even thinking about capitulation. Blackshirts, reconstitute your battalions that have undertaken such heroic deeds! You, young Fascists, join the divisions that so bravely fought in Birlgobi; you, aviators that have counteracted so well the enemy's attacks on our cities; and you, Fascist women, become once more our people's moral and material support, of which he is so much in need of! Peasants, workers, craftsmen! The coming state will be your state. Defend it so no one can, never again, put it in peril. Our valor, our faith and our will, will give Italy a new future, and together with it, new possibilities of life and its place in the sun. Convert this hope in an unbreakable certainty! Long live Italy! Long live the new Fascist Republican Party!

V
The Verona "Manifest"

The Verona Manifest, name by which became known the programmatic declaration of the FRP[72], was balloted in a Sunday, 14th of November, 1943, at the Party's congress in Verona.

The 18 points

Regarding the internal constitutional matters:

1. A Constitutive Assembly shall be convoked, sovereign power of popular origin, to declare the Monarchy's abolition and the solemn condemnation of its last king as a traitor and a deserter, and, once that the Social Republic has been proclaimed, it shall nominate its leader.

2. The Constitutive Assembly is formed by representatives of all the Syndical associations and administrative circumscriptions, including those representing the occupied provinces through the refugee delegations in the free territory.
Furthermore it must include the representations of the combatants, of the prisoners of war through those handicapped repatriated; of the expatriated Italians, of the magistracy, of the universities or of whatever corporation or institute, whose participation may contribute to make from the Constitutive Assembly the synthesis of all the Nation's valors.

3. The Republican Constitution shall assure the citizen's - soldier, worker or tax payer – right to control and evaluate in a responsible manner the performance of the public administration. Every five years, the citizen will be called upon to choose the Republic's leader.
No citizen, either if caught in the act of committing an offence or by coercive preventive measures, may be incarcerated for more than seven days, without the correspondent judicial order. Furthermore, with the

---
[72] Fascist Republican Party.

exception of *in flagrante delicto*, it shall be required a judicial warrant to undertake any house search. When exercising its attributions, the magistracy shall act with full independence.

4. The negative outcome of the electoral experience already undertaken in Italy, as well as the partial negative experience in what concerns the electoral proceedings, too rigidly hierarchized, give way to a solution that conciliates the opposing demands. A mixed system (for instance, popular election of the Parliament representatives and ministers, nomination by the [sole] head of both the Republic and the government, and, in the Party, elections for the Fasci, subjected to ratification, and appointment of the directorate by the Duce) seems to be the most advisable.

5. There will be a unique competent organization for the people's political education.
Inside the Party, constituted by combatants and sympathizers, there should be an organism of absolute political purity, worthy of becoming the safeguard of the Revolutionary idea.

The Party's membership card shall not be asked to fill whatsoever work post or position.

6. The Republic's religion is the Catholic, Apostolic and Roman one. Any other cult that does not oppose the laws shall be respected.

7. All people belonging to the Hebrew race are to be considered as foreigners. For the duration of this war they are considered as belonging to an enemy nationality.

Revolutionary Fascism

Regarding the foreign policy:

8. "The essential goal of the external policy must be the unity, the independence and the territorial integrity of the Fatherland in its maritime and alpine limits designated by nature, bloody sacrifice and History; borders that are threatened by the enemy due to the invasion and by the promises made to the governments that sought refuge in London. Another essential goal will consist in having recognized the necessity of indispensable vital spaces for a people of 45 million inhabitants that are located in an insufficient area to nourish them.

Furthermore, such policy shall be adopted for the setting of a European community, federating all nations that accept the following fundamental principles:

a) Elimination of the centennial British intrigues in our continent.

b) Abolition of the internal [European] Capitalist system, opposition to the Plutocracies.

c) Valorization, on behalf of the European and Autochthonous peoples, of Africa's natural resources, absolutely respecting those peoples, especially the Muslims, that, like in Egypt, are nationally and civilly organized.

Regarding Social matters:

9. The basis and primordial object of the Social Republic is the manual, technical and intellectual labor in all of its manifestations.

10. Private property, fruit of work and of personal savings - an integral part of the human personality - is guaranteed by the state. Nevertheless, it may not disintegrate the moral and physic personality of others, through the exploitation of their work.

11. As for the national economy, all of those activities not strictly comprehended in the private interest scope but that by their dimension or function encompass the area of collective interest belong to the very own state´s sphere of action. The public services, and therefore by nature the war production, are to be run by the state through parastatal entities.

12. In every company (industrial, private, parastatal and state-owned) the technicians and blue collar workers delegations will cooperate intimately - being directly acquainted with its management - in the task of setting equitable wages, as in the just distribution of the profits between the reserve fund, the actionist capital revenues and the workers participation in such revenues.

In some companies, this can be achieved by giving wider prerogatives to factory commissions, already in place. As for others the administration boards may be substituted by company boards composed by technicians, blue collar workers and a state representative. Finally it may also be implemented through a para-Syndical cooperative.

13. In agriculture, the landowner's private initiative shall be limited only by lack of initiative itself. The non-cultivated lands and the ill administrated properties can be expropriated and inclusively parceled and handed over to rural workers as direct cultivators, or become cooperative, para-Syndical or parastatal properties, according to the needs of the agricultural economy. All of this is already abridged by the laws by now in vigor, to which enforcement the Party and the Syndical organizations should concur to give the necessary stimulus.

14. The direct cultivators, craftsmen, professionals and artists are entitled to make the most of their own productive activities, individually, familiarly or in groups, obliged only to hand over the amount of products established by law and to submit the rates of the services rendered to control.

15. House holding is not only an [abstract] right to property, but a [concrete] right to ownership. The Party includes in its program the setting up of a national institution for the people's housing projects. Which, absorbing the existent institutes and widening its action to the maximum shall facilitate house ownership to worker's families of whatever category, both by direct construction of new lodgments and the gradual amortization of the existent ones. One must emphasize the general principle that lease holding - once that capital has been reimbursed and the just profit paid for -

Revolutionary Fascism

constitutes an ownership title.

As a primordial obligation, the Institute shall deal with the problems derived of destructions caused by war, seizing and distributing vacant premises and provisional facilities.

16. The worker shall be mandatory enrolled, with full rights, in his area of expertise union; this does not prevent his transference to another [union] whenever he possesses the necessary requirements. The unions converge into a unique confederation in which are included all workers, technicians and professionals, excluding the owners that aren't either managers or technicians. This one shall be denominated as General Confederation of Work, Technique and Arts.

The employees of the state industrial companies and of the public services shall form unions, like the rest of the workers. All of the welfare laws instituted by the Fascist regime during the last twenty years are hereby declared effective. The Labor Chart constitutes, to the letter- both in its consecration as in its spirit - the point of departure towards a future life.

17. In the present circumstances the Party deems as necessary an immediate readjustment of the workers' salaries, through the adoption of national minimum wages and immediate local revisions, concerning above all the lower and medium rank employees, both private and stately. In order to avoid that such measures were to be ineffective and, at a later time, harmful to all it shall be sought that throughout stock management, within cooperatives and private companies, a broad "welfare" aid and the seizure of businesses - culprits of past infractions, from thereon placed under parastatal or cooperative management - it may became possible to pay a part of the wages in victuals at the official price rate. Only through this shall we achieve the stabilization of the prices and of the currency and the market's restoration. As in what concerns the black market, we ask that the speculators, the same as the traitors and the defeatists, fall within the extraordinary tribunals' jurisdiction and may be convicted to the death penalty.

18. With this preamble to the Constitutive Assembly, the Party demonstrates that he is not merely trying to get close to the people, but that he is at the people's side. At their own end the Italian people must be aware that there is a sole mean to defend its yesterday's, today's and tomorrow's conquests: to refuse the Anglo-American Plutocracies' enslaving invasion, whose goal is - innumerous signs have already revealed it to us - to heighten the distressed and pitiful life of the Italians. There is but a way to attain all of the social goals: to fight, to work, to win.

Revolutionary Fascism

VI
The Socialization, law of the Italian Social Republic

January the 13th, 1944, the cabinet council had already approved a fundamental premise for the creation of Italy's economic new structure, in which it gave a decisive importance to the state's intervention in the economy, altogether granting labor a privileged position with rights and responsibilities not yet achieved. The "premise" was presented by Mussolini.

The 12th of February, 1944, cabinet council approved the "Socialization" bill of law; its main goals could be summarized as follows:

1. The armed struggle is to be accompanied by the reinforcement of the political ideal;
2. Enforcement of the Mussolinian conception on subjects such as; a much higher Social Justice, a more equitable distribution of wealth and the participation of labor in the state's life;
3. To normalize the internal situation, regarding the relationships between capital and labor, by conceding to its production factors the rights, duties and responsibilities that correspond to each one, according with the state's life itself;
4. To fully grasp the social function, the responsibility and the persona of the company's manager in what regards the productive activity of his organization and the social relationships in the life of the company itself, basing in objective concepts the valorization and the merits of each individual;
5. To increase, through a well organized production and a normalization of the company's life, the productive capacity of each one of the sections, thus creating the most efficient instrument possible to solve the warlike problems, with the purpose of contributing – thru the Italian economy effort - to the Axis [war effort] and to the coming post-war era;
6. To counteract the Communist conception that culminates in a state's Capitalism, in which each of the production factors is deprived of representation and participation rights in the state's life, with the Fascist and National Socialist one that aims to drive capital and labor to cooperate in the state's life;
7. To safeguard and increase the private initiative within the sanctioned principles of the Labor's Chart orbit, antidote both against the Communist

Party by one hand, and the Plutocratic by the other;

8. To set up a new Order offering the people the possibility to construct its own tomorrow and to conquest its place in the European international scene after the Axis's victory.

To these goals corresponds the disposition submitted to the approval of the Cabinet Council, that empowers in form of law the three guidelines that are inscribed in the programmatic basis approved by the same council in the late 11th of January: instating of labor in company management, transferring to state property of those companies that by their importance surpass the private scope, limitation of capital revenues and participation of labor in such revenues. Of these guidelines, the first one is considered to be the most important, given that it establishes, as a general criterion, that labor forces are to get in touch with the core of the production mechanism and actively participate in its life through their own representatives. This criterion is to be considered as the revolutionary axis of the company's new structure, as state ownership of any given companies only constitutes, by itself, a form of state Capitalism, a burocratization of the economic process, if it is to be confined to the control of productive activity by public powers. But the transference to state property of some determined and numerically limited companies, conceived by us, fits the requirements of the country's economic structure general Socialization process and constitutes a more advanced and integral form of Socialization of those sectors predominantly of interest to the community, requiring of her to assume in a direct way its ownership and control, excluding the intervention of particularistic forces and interests. This can surely be achieved through state property, which is the representative of the community, but also through the integral and direct participation of labor in its management.

The same can be said of the other guideline that inspires the disposition submitted to the Council's approval: labor's participation in the revenues. The later can neither be conceived nor can it be implemented if labor is not to acquire knowledge and consciousness of the company's productive activity, of its problems, of its demands and of its possibilities, fully assuming the form of a collaborator in the very own company's management. The predominant importance of the concept of Socialization explains both the entitlement of the law as the systematic order that has been followed in it, therefore the title referring to the company's Socialized administration precedes those that refer to the transferring of companies to state ownership and the determination and distribution of revenues.

VII
Companies' Socialization Bill of Law

Hereunder is the Bill of Law on Socialization as approved by the Cabinet Council:

The Duce of the Social Italian Republic
Given the Labor Chart;
Given the project of the new social-economic structure, approved by the Cabinet Council in the 13th of January, 1944;
By proposal of the Corporative Economy minister and with and in full agreement with the Finance and the Justice Ministers,

Decrees that:

(Title one)

Art. 1. Company's management.
The company's management, either state-owned or of private property, is hereby Socialized. In it labor assumes a direct role. The Socialized companies functioning is regulated by the present bill of law, by the statute or regulation of each company, by civil code norms and by the special laws insofar as they do not contradict the present dispositions.

Art. 2. Organisms of company's management.
The organisms for the company's management are:

a) For the private companies assuming the form of shareholders societies or for limited liability societies with a minimum of capital of one million: the company's head, the assembly, the administration board and the Syndical College;

b) For the private companies that assume other legal form of society: the company's head and the administration board;

c) For the individual private companies: the company head and the management board;

d) For the companies owned by the state: the company head, the administration board and the Syndical College.

Section I
Private property companies' administration

Chapter I. Social capital companies' management

Art. 3. Organisms of the Shareholders societies and of the limited liability societies.

In the shareholders societies and in the limited liability ones, with a minimum of one million in capital, the elected representatives of the company's workers that take part in the collegial administration organisms are: blue collar workers, white collar workers, technicians and managers.

Art. 4. Assembly, management council and Syndical College.

By virtue of the dispositions in vigor in article 2,368 of the Civil Code, and following articles, on its regulatory constitution, the workers representatives are to participate in the assembly with a number of votes equal to the one of the intervened capital.

The assembly nominates an administration board formed in half by the associate's representatives, and in the other half by the worker's representatives. Furthermore, the assembly nominates a Syndical College, whose members must include among them, at least, a titular trustee and a substitute, proposed by the workers representatives in agreement with the dispositions established in the Civil Code for Syndical Colleges.

Art. 5. Voting.

When of the voting, in the assembly or in the administration board, will prevail - if a tie should occur - the vote of the company's head that, by law, presides the former social organisms.

Art. 6. Management council of societies that are neither of shareholding type nor of limited liability.

In the societies that are not comprised in Art. 3 and that do possess a minimum of one million in capital or that have at least 100 workers, the management council will be filled by partners and, in equal number, by elected representatives of the company's workers.

Art. 7. Management council powers.

The management council of the social capital private companies is submitted to a periodical and systematic examination of its technical, economical and financial management.

a) It deliberates on all matters related with the company's life, on the production's development orientation within the framework of the national plan established by the competent state's organisms;

b) It exposes its reasoning on the work contracts stipulation to the Syndical associations encadred in the General Confederation of Work, Technique and Arts, and on any other subject inherent to the discipline and tutelage of labor and of the company;

c) In general, it exercises within the company all of the rights conferred by the statute and those inscribed in the valid laws regarding the administrators whenever they do not counteract the dispositions of the present regulation;

d) It balances the company's books and proposals the benefits distributions, abiding to the dispositions of the current regulation and of the Civil Code.

Art. 8. Management council members' prerogatives.

The members of the management council elected by the workers are not obliged to give oath.

Art. 9. The company's head.

In the shareholders societies and in those of limited liability with a minimum of a million in capital, the company head is elected among the associates, according to the modalities inscribed in the constitution proceedings statute and regulation of the above mentioned societies.

Art. 10. Powers of the company's head.

The company's head convenes the assembly presiding it, in addition: he presides the administration board; represents the company in its dealings with third parties. He has the responsibility and the rights appointed by the Art. 21, and following articles, and all of the powers that are assigned to him in the statute, as also the ones inscribed in the current laws, whenever these do not counteract the dispositions of the present regulation.

Chapter II. Individual capital companies' administration.

Art. 11. Management council.

In the individual companies, whenever the invested capital reaches a million and the number of workers a hundred, there is to be a management council composed by, at least, three members elected accordingly to the company's regulation: blue collar workers, white collar workers, technicians and managers.

Art. 12. The company's head and powers of the management council.

In the individual companies, the entrepreneur, that assumes the juridical persona as head of the company with the responsibilities and duties established in the Art. 21 and following, is assisted in the company's management by the management council, who shall adjust its activity to the state's Social policy guidelines. The entrepreneur head of the company shall periodically convene, at least once a month, the council to submit to it the matters related with the company's production, and annually, when of the balancing of the company's books, for its approval and benefits distribution.

Section II
Management of the state owned companies

Art. 13. The company's head.

The head of a company owned by the state is nominated by decree of the Corporative Economy minister in agreement with the Finance minister, having been previously designated by the Finance and Management Institute, chosen among the members of the company's administration board or among other elements of the same company or of companies belonging to the same production branch that offer special guarantees of recognized technical or administrative guarantees. The head of the company has the responsibility and the duties appointed by the Art. 21 and following, its powers are to be determined by each company's statute.

Art. 14. Administration board.
The administration board shall be presided by the head of the company and composed by elected representatives of the various categories of the company's workers: blue collar workers, technicians, white collar workers and managers, as well as a representative proposed by the Finance and Management Institute and appointed by the Finance minister. The election proceedings and the number of members of the board shall be established by the company's statute. The members of the board shall not receive any sort of repayment by their management, with the exception of allowances to cover their expenses.

Art. 15. Powers of the company's board.
In what concerns the powers of the state owned companies' administration boards, they shall abide by the norms inscribed in the previous Art. 7.

Art. 16. Syndical college.
The Syndical College of the companies owned by the state shall be constituted by a decree of the Corporative Economy minister, in full agreement with the Finance minister and by proposal of the Finance and Management Institute, commissioned to establish the trustees' repayment.

Art. 17. Balance of the books and distribution of the benefits.
The balance of the books in state owned companies and the benefits distribution project, the augmentation and reduction of capital, as well as fusions, concentrations, selection and liquidation of state owned companies, are to be carried out by proposal of the Credit and Companies Institute, having heard the administration board of the interested companies, with previous approval of the Corporative Economy minister

and in agreement with the Finance minister and the other interested ministers.

Section III
Common dispositions to the previous sections

Art. 18. State owned companies constitutive and statutory acts.

The foundational acts and the statutes of the state owned companies, as well as their correspondent modifications, are approved by decree of the Corporative Economy minister, in agreement with the Finance minister.

Art. 19. Statutes and regulations of private property companies.

Starting from June 30, 1944, all of the private capital companies shall precede to adapt their statutes to the norms inscribed in the present decree. Their statutes and regulations shall be submitted within thirty days to the homologation of the competent territorial tribunal, who, having confirmed its regularity and correspondence with the present decree and other laws in vigor on the subject, shall ordain their transcription on the companies' registration [office].

Art. 20. Election modality of the workers representatives.

The workers representatives called upon to take part in the Socialized companies' organisms, be those owned by the state or by privates, are elected by secret vote by all the company's workers: blue collar workers, white collar workers, technicians and managers. The candidates are promulgated through lists made out by the municipal unions of the respective branch, in twice the number of the representatives to elect and proportionally to the company's respective categories.

Art. 21. Responsibilities of the head of the companies.

The head of the company, be those owned by the state or by privates, is personally responsible before the state of the company's production development and may be replaced or discharged according with the following articles and in the cases sanctioned by the law in vigor when his activity does not comply with the demands of the general production plans and of the state's social policy guidelines.

Art. 22. Replacement of the head of a company owned by the state.

In a company owned by the state, the replacement of the company's head is part of the assignments of the Corporative Economy minister - in full agreement with the Finance minister, having heard other potentially interested ministers - by its own initiative or by proposal either of the Credit and Administration Institute, the administration board or of the trustees [college], with previous opportune confirmation.

Art. 23. Replacement of a private social capital company's head.

In the shareholder societies, the replacement of the company's head is carried out by deliberation of the assembly. In all other social capital companies, the replacement of the company's head regulates itself by the foundational statutes or regulations, although it may be also promoted by the administration board, through the same preceding inscribed in the article 24 and following regarding the individual capital private companies. It is within the Corporative Economy minister power scope to proceed to the substitution of the company's head whenever this one demonstrates not to possess the sense of responsibility or fails to comply with the duties appointed in Art. 21.

Art. 24. Replacement of the individual capital company's head.

In the individual capital private companies, the entrepreneur, head of the company, can only be replaced by a previous verdict of the labor magistracy, organism cognizable to enquire about the responsibilities. The declaration of responsibilities may be promoted either by the company's administration board or by the Credit and Administration Institute, given an interest of the latter in the company, or by the Cooperative Economy minister, through an official request to the area's Court of Appeals state procurator.

Art. 25. Proceedings of the labor magistracy.

The labor magistracy, having heard the entrepreneur, the company's administration board, or the Credit and Administration Institute, and having appreciated the probationary body of proof, declares through a verdict the responsibility of the entrepreneur. Against the verdict it is admissible a disempowerment appeal, sanctioned in the Civil Procedure Code, Art. 426.

Art. 26. Sanctions against the head of the company.

Once the verdict that declares the entrepreneurs responsibility has been delivered, the Corporative Economy minister shall undertake those measures judged to be the most convenient in the case, intrusting, if necessary, the company's administration to a cooperative formed by the workers of such a company.

Art. 27. Preventive measures.

Whenever the application of the precedent articles is still pending, the Corporative Economy minister may suspend, by decree, the activities of the entrepreneur head of the company and appoint a commissar to provisionally manage the company.

Art. 28. Administration board responsibilities.

Whenever the management company board, be that owned by the state or private [capital], displays insufficient sense of responsibility in the fulfillment of the outlined duties to adapt the company's activity to the demands of the Republic's social policy and production plans, the minister of Corporative Economy, in full agreement with the Finance minister, may decide, given the probationary evidence, on the board's dissolution and in the appointment of a commissar to provisionally manage the company. The Corporative Economy minister intervention may be carried out by his own initiative or by request of the Credit and Administration Institute, of the head of the company, of the assembly or of the representatives of the union.

Art. 29. Penal sanctions.

To the head of the company and to the members of its administration board, be that state owned or private, may be applied the sanctions inscribed in the laws concerning entrepreneurs, partners and administrators of commercial societies.

(Title II)

Section IV
Company's head and administrator responsibilities

Art. 30. Transferring of companies to state ownership.

The ownership of companies whose activity is deemed as of interest to the country's political and economical independence, as well as those who provide raw materials, energy and indispensable services to the normal development of social life, may be assumed by the state according to the present decree normative. Whenever the company is to be considered as having several productive activities, the state may assume only a part of the ownership of such a company. Furthermore, the state may participate in private companies' capital.

Art. 31. Proceedings to company transference to state ownership.

Those companies that eventually are to be transferred to state ownership shall be appointed by a decree of the head of state, having heard the ministers' cabinet, by proposal of the Corporative Economy minister, in full agreement with the Finance minister.

Art. 32. Syndicate jurisdiction, appointment of the heads of the unions and of the government commissars.

By force of the previous article decree's enactment and by decrees to follow, the companies that are to be transferred to state ownership are to be under the union's scope according to the proceeding inscribed in the law 1,100, of July 17, 1942. The company's provisional management may be entrusted to one of its administrators acting as a government commissar.

Art. 33. Annulment of the affairs that modify the capital's title deeds.

There are to be considered null all businesses among private parts that, in whatever case, modify the property relationship regarding the shareholders title deeds constituting the capital of the companies appointed to be transferred to state ownership, held from the date on of the disposition's, deciding the ownership transference, entry into force.

Art. 34. Capital administration of the state owned companies.

The capital of companies who have been transferred to state ownership is to be administered by the Credit and Administration Institute, public office entity with its own juridical persona. The Institute's constitution and the approval of the correspondent statute are to be carried out through separate dispositions.

Art. 35. Task of the Credit and Administration Institute.

The Credit and Administration Institute controls the company's activities inscribed in Art. 30, according to the Corporative Economy minister guidelines and, furthermore it manages the state's interests in private companies.

Art. 36. Transformation of paid-in capital.

The paid-in capital already invested in companies that are to be transferred to state ownership is replaced by paid-in credits issued by the Credit and Administration Institute accordingly to the following articles.

Art. 37. Paid-in capital transfer value.

The substitution of the paid-in capital, already invested in a company that is to be transferred to state ownership, by Credit and Administration Institute titles are to be undertaken considering the full amount of the already mentioned paid-in capital's real value.

Art. 38. Determination of the paid-in capital value.

Whenever there is a disagreement with the company's administrators the paid-in capital real value of the companies that are to be transferred to state ownership shall be determined by a Corporative Economy minister decree, in full agreement with the Finance minister, by proposal of the Credit and Administration Institute. This Corporate Economy minister decree may be the subject of an appeal, within 60 days of its publication, to the state Cabinet by either the company's administrators or a number of partners that represents at least the 10th part of the social capital.

Art. 39. Features of the Credit and Administration Institute titles.

The Credit and Administration Institute titles are nominative, negotiable and transferable and of variable revenues. They are issued in distinct series correspondent to the various production sectors. The revenue of each one of these series shall be determined annually by the Savings and Credit Exercise Protection Ministers Committee, by proposal of the Credit and Administration Institute taking in consideration the development of the correspondent production sectors.

Art. 40. Titles negotiability limitations.

The negotiability limitation of the Credit and Administration Institute titles, issued in substitution of the paid-in capital, and inscription in the Credit Institute ledgers of the holders of such titles, without its material consignation, is hereby delegated to the Savings and Credit Exercise Protection Ministers Committee.

Art. 41. Transfer modalities to state ownership.

In the decree that enacts the transference to state ownership are established the executive norms, the modality and necessary and opportune terms to the capital's transference to the state and for the appointment and distribution of the Credit and Administration Institute titles to those who are entitled to them.

Title VIII
Shares and capital

Art. 42. Revenues assignation.

The company's net revenues depend on the balancing of the books resulting from the application of the Civil Code norms, based on an administrative accounting that may come to be successively unified through opportune legal disposition.

Art. 43. Capital revenues.

After the legal consignations to the reserve and once that has been established the eventual special reserves in favor of the enacted statutes and regulations, a remuneration shall be granted to the company's invested capital in a maximum amount set by the Savings and Credit Exercise Protection Ministers Committee production sectors.

Art. 44. Revenues assignation to the workers.

The remaining revenues once made the previous article referred assignations, shall be distributed among the workers: blue collar workers, white collar workers, technicians and managers. This assignation shall take place bearing in mind the remunerations that each one of them receives during a year's time. All things considered, the amount distributed may not exceed, in whatever case, thirty percent of the workers [yearlong] salary net total corresponding to the [accounting] exercise. The surplus shall be destined to a compensation Savings Bank, administrated by the Credit and Administration Institute, and destined to social and productive goals. In a aside disposition, the Corporative Economy minister, in full agreement with the Finance minister, shall approve the regulation of such a Savings Bank.

Art. 45. Revenues share.

In the individual capital companies, the revenues share assigned in benefice of the workers shall be proportional to a given percentage of the revenues comprehended in the movable assets tax base[73].

This given decree, that shall be published in the "Official Gazette of the Italian Social Republic" and inscribed, with the correspondent state seal, in the official collection of laws and decrees, shall come into effect in the day designated by the correspondent decree of the Italian Social Republic Duce's.

---

[73] Translator's note: In this case the exploration income tax.

Revolutionary Fascism

VIII
The workers and Socialization

The state's social reform was closely followed and coupled with the Syndical one. The decree number 853 that created the General (or sole) Confederation of Work, Technique and Arts, dated of December 20, 1943, was complemented by a ministerial decree on March 1, 1944. The passage from the old to the new Syndical state of affairs was motive for an intense legislative activity. The new Syndical order was definitely established by the decree number 3 of January 18, 1945.

The reaction to the Mussolinian reform was immediate. In many factories orders of the day were voted, meetings were held and motions approved.

The representatives of the Burgo paper factories, gathered at Milan, *"recognize in the Socialization a decisive phase of the Proletarian revolution, which, after having been fought off for more than a century by blind Capitalism, warmonger and class hate fomenter, emerges today in the Italian Social Republic, in History's most grievous moment, to attain and ensure the Nation's rebirth"*.

In Turin, the Fiat's internal commissions rose against the sabotage intents of the CLN elements, publishing, in turn, another appeal: *"it should be considered as a fraud, to the Fiat workers disadvantage, the scheme undertaken against the most revolutionary law that has ever been promulgated in the workers behalf: the Socialization Act... the Socialization has but one enemy: Capitalism. And those who oppose it are inspired, paid for and guided by the occult powers of Capitalism. By the first time in the History of social life, the workers find themselves as absolute masters of their own faith. And they are not willing to waste this occasion only because Capitalism disfavors it."*

Already in the 10th of April, 1945, (one must attend to the date), the representatives of Milan's factories commissions, at the end of a meeting in the Workers House, *"invite the government of the Italian Social Republic to act with inflexible energy against the heads of those companies that haven't presented the statutes in due time, committing themselves to develop an effective propaganda and control campaign, calling to the fulfillment of the*

117

present hour duty by all of the workers of the remaining Italian provinces, so as to achieve a full realization of the Socialization principles, in behalf of Labor".

Later on, Mussolini will include in the already mentioned "Corrispondenza" some of the most characteristic manifestations of his thought in social matters from 1919 onwards: "*Consequentially, it is absolutely useless that the short memory Italians are to adopt the attitude of the one that falls from the clouds and is swept by the most authentic of surprises in what regards the Socialization fundamental disposition*". Further on in the same "Corrispondenza", Mussolini declared that "*Fascism does not renegate its 20 year old origins, but it remits itself to its most genuine essence, eliminating the external obstacles and the internal resistances that obstruct to the realization of its highest social goals*", and ends by saying that "*it is indeed a new milestone that is left behind, but one that we do not disclaim, of a path in which we have strenuously hiked on...*"

IX
Speech to the "Resega" Division

This speech was delivered by Mussolini in the 14th of October, 1944, before a group of Milanese Fascist veterans and of officers of the Black Brigade "Resega", that had adopted the name of Aldo Resega, governor of the Republican Fascist Party in Milan, murdered in December 18, 1943. It was in this speech that Mussolini launched the Northern slogan: "Italy - Republic - Socialization":

...In the Verona meeting, the Republican Fascist Party has set up its guidelines. If the vicissitudes of war have delayed the application of some of those that does not mean that they have been changed. They are still in vigor. In the moments of high moral and political tension, it is necessary that the slogans be few and extremely clear.

However there are still those who ask of us: "what do you want?" We answer with three words that summon up our entire program.

Here they are: Italy, Republic, Socialization.

For us, enemies of abstract Patriotism, both calculating and circumstantial, and because of that inclined to compromising and even to defection, Italy means honor, and honor means faith in the given promise - indispensable reputation title both for the individual as for the peoples; and faith in the given promise means collaboration with the ally, both in work as in struggle.

Bear in mind - and History confirms it - that the traitors, in politics or in war, are used, but also despised.

And precisely in this moment, when Germany commits itself into a supreme struggle and 80 millions of Germans have converted themselves in 80 millions of soldiers, devoted to a superhuman resistance effort; it's precisely in this moment that the enemies anticipate - halfway between hope and illusion - a victory that they shall not achieve, because Germany will never capitulate, because that for Germany to capitulate would be the same as "dying" politically, morally and physically; it is in this moment that we reaffirm our full and total solidarity with National Socialist Germany that is the Germany that fights with a courage and a valor that one could denominate as "Romans" and that has brought upon them an admired recognition inclusively from those enemies that still haven't been completely blinded or turned into brutes by hate.

All of this is clear for everyone. And it is, in turn, the indeclinable object of the Italian Republic. The series of treasons, discrediting the Savoy - from Carlos Alberto to Vittorio Emanuele III- have ended with the overthrowing of the Monarchy. Our Italy is a Republican one. To the North of the Apennines we have the Italian Social Republic. This Republic shall be defended inch by inch to its last province, to its last village, to its last farmhouse. Whatever may be the vicissitudes of war in our territory, the idea of the Republic founded by Fascism has already forever entered in the spirit and in the people's ways. The program's third word, Socialization, it's nothing but the consequence of the first two: Italy and Republic. Socialization is no other thing than the implantation of an Italian Socialism, humane, ours and possible; and I say "ours", as far as it makes of work the economy's sole motive, refusing the mechanical leverages inexistent in nature and impossible in History.

All of those whose soul is cleared of prejudices and of seditious sectarianisms may recognize themselves in the trinomial: Italy, Republic, Socialization. With this we intend to summon to the political scene the best elements of our working people.

The September capitulation means the shameful liquidation of the bourgeoisie globally considered as the ruling class. The spectacle offered by the former has been scandalous. There were incredible cases of abjection, sordid demonstrations of selfishness dismissing as if worthless the highest social and national values.

As always, those who have subordinated their feelings and opinions to the war development, are only worthy of sympathy, and in some cases of despise. Many people's state of mind, of every social conditions, do without the positive exam of the state of affairs, who, by its complexity and universality, cannot be judged upon momentary feelings provoked by the absorbent enemy propaganda.

Not only Germany will never capitulate, because it can't capitulate, given that the enemies are set upon to annihilate it both stately and racially, but also because it has still many arrows in its bow, apart from what we

Revolutionary Fascism

could call: the unanimous decision and the iron will of its people.

The enemies do not conceal that they are in haste. We are aware of our pains, many as they are, but is there anyone so candidly naïf to believe that in England, in Russia and in the United States all goes in the best possible way? Are we to believe that in England there is not a considerable numerous group of intelligent persons that ask themselves if it is worthy to engage in a battle against the so-called German imperialism, losing hundreds of thousands of men, as well as all its holdings in the Far East, to consolidate a Slavic imperialism that already holds in its fist all of Europe from the Vistula to the Baltic and - not a flattering detail for London - to the Mediterranean? Are we to believe that we do not already hear voices proclaiming that the absurd and arrogant Casablanca's formula "of unconditional surrender" be revised as to not provoke an ulterior sacrifice of the life of millions? The greatest carnage of all times has a name: Democracy, word that conceals the Zionist Capitalist voracity that wants to undertake the world's scientific exploitation through the ruin of mankind and the catastrophe of civilization.

Therefore the inner acknowledgment of this truth means to realize that, in a given moment, events shall take another course and that war's future development - in which science will play the main role - shall drown all of the enemy's victory forecasts. In this stage of the war we declare that we must: eliminate all of the enemy's accomplices in our mist and call to our ranks all of the Italians that accept our program's trinomial.

Come what may, we shall not modify not even a sole line of the program that today addressing thee, comrades of the Black Brigades - expression and honor of the pristine Fascio - I wanted to sketch out.

Under the protection of foreign and mercenary bayonets, the unconditional surrender men, that is to say, infamous and cowards, strive in vain in their persecution of Fascists and Fascism. With it they amount to nothing than to give testimony of its unbreakable continuity. Their parties are artificially based in a merely negative entailment: Fascism's radical and iconoclastic persecution.

Their attitude is due to their confirmation that the alleged corpse is nonetheless still alive; that it still lingers in the air that they breath, in all that they stumble upon with at each step, in the indelible markings both material and spiritual that Fascism has left everywhere. No human force can erase from History that what has already gone down in History as a reality and a faith.

For twenty years now, in peace and in war, in Italy, in Europe and in Africa tenths of thousands of Fascists have fallen, the blossom of the Italian race, next to their black banners. Fascism's heroic expression, they constitute its immortal testimony and safeguard.

Deliver to the Milanese comrades, along with my salutation, the echo of my certainty in the victorious conclusion for Italy and Europe of this colossal civilizational clash that goes by the name of Fascism.

X
The Lyrical's address

The Milanese Lyrical Theatre address (16th of December, 1944), is the most important political speech of all that Mussolini gave after his return to government. The ministers themselves and the remaining German and Italian authorities were not given notice of it until the very last moment. The welcoming that Milan gave the Duce was a reminder of times gone by; the Duce himself couldn't help to be moved by it. The address had a wide echo, and gave place to plenty of commentaries, inclusively in enemy countries. Here is the unabridged text of the address that was titled as "The Lyrical Address".

Comrades, dear Milanese comrades: I do without any sort of preamble and without further a due I will head straight to my addresses' core theme.

After sixteen months from the imposed and accepted surrendering date, accordingly with the Democratic and criminal formula of Casablanca, the events importance places us, once more, before this question: who has betrayed? Who has suffered in an immediate manner the consequences of the betrayal? Let us be clear on this: I do not intend to pass judgment on matters of historical revisionism nor do I, even less, intend to justify myself.

I have been accused, by a certain neutral newspaper, but I refuse it in the most categorical way, both as in what concerns its content as by the very source of which it originates.

Who has betrayed? The surrendering announced in the 8th of September, 1943, was desired by the Monarchy, by the court's entourage, by the Plutocratic circles of the Italian bourgeoisie, by well determined Clerical powers occasionally united to those of the Freemasonry, by the General Headquarters that no longer believed in victory and that gathered around Badoglio. In May, [1943,] precisely in the 15th, the former king wrote down in his diary - that recently came into our possession - that he needed, more than ever, to "get rid of" the alliance with Germany. The surrender was ordered by the former king, without a shadow of a doubt; its executioner was Badoglio.

But for one to arrive to the 8th of September, it is necessary to have previously experienced the 25th of July, that is to say, to undertake the coup d'état and the regime's change.

The surrendering justification, namely the impossibility to further continue the war, was debunked forty days later, in the 13th of October, with the declaration of war on Germany, declaration not merely symbolic, given that from that point on a collaboration was initiated - even if only in the rearguard and in labor activities - between Badoglian Italy and the Allies; not to mention that the fleet, totally constructed by Fascism, has switched sides en bloc in order to immediately start to operate with the enemy fleets. Peace was not in order, though, but, through the above mentioned co-belligerence, the continuation of war; peace was not in order, all of the nation's entire territory was converted into an immense battlefield, that is to say in a immense field of ruins; peace was not in order, rather Italian boats and Italian troops were supposed to participate in the war against Japan.

Therefore, the one that suffered the most as a consequence of treason was mainly the Italian people.

One can say that regarding the relations with the German ally, the Italian people has not committed treason. With exception of a few cases, the army sections disbanded without resisting the disarmament orders of the German authorities. Important army contingents, deployed outside of the metropolitan territory, inclusively the aviation, immediately stood by the side of the German forces - and one must bear in mind that we are speaking of tens of thousands of men - all of the Militia formations - with the exception of a Corsican battalion - stood by the German side to the very last moment.

The so called P.44 plan that shall be discussed in the imminent generals' trial and that foresaw the front's debacle such as it was prepared by the king and Badoglio, was not carried out by the commanding officers, and this is proven in the lawsuit that was moved, in Bonomi's Italy, against a group of generals that did not abide to the orders of such a plan. The same did the army commanders deployed outside the borders.

If such commanders avoided the worst, that is to say, the extreme infamy that would have resulted from backstabbing the one that for three years had been their ally, their conduct from the national point of view has been disastrous: obeying to the voice of conscience and honor, they should have switched sides, with all their belongings. This way they could have maintained our territorial and political positions; our flag would not have been lowered in lands were so much Italian blood had been shed; the armed forces would have conserved their organic constitution; it could have been avoided that hundreds of thousands of soldiers were to be forcibly interned [in German concentration camps], thus avoiding their great sufferings, above all moral; our ally would not have been overloaded by the imposition of new and unexpected military problems that were to influence the strategic development of war.

These are the specific responsibilities of the Italian people.

Furthermore, one should recognize, that the treasons of the Summer of 1944 gave place to even more shameful displays, once that the Romanians, Bulgarians and Finnish, after having ignominiously capitulated, specially the Bulgarians, without having shot a single rifle bullet, have dismantled the front within 24 hours and attacked, with all the mobilized forces, the German units, thus converting their retreat in a difficult and bloody operation.

In this case treason has reached perfection in the most repugnant meaning of the word.

The Italian people is, however, the one who has intervened the less and that has suffered to a point that I have no doubt in qualifying as over-human. It is not sufficient. I must ad that while a part of the Italian people has accepted - by unconsciousness or tiredness - the surrendering, the other part of it has taken Germany's side.

It is time to say to the Italians, to the German comrades and to the Japanese comrades, that the contribution made by the Italian Republic to the common cause from September, 1943, onwards - in spite of the circumstantial reduction of the Republic's territory - is much more important than one is commonly to believe.

I cannot, by evident reasons, go to the length of detailing the numbers of such contribution, complex in its utmost degree - both in an economic as military point of view -, made by Italy. Our collaboration with the Reich in soldiers and workers can be represented by this number: 786,000 men, according to data gathered until the 30th of September. This is an undisputable data, given that it proceeds of German source. Furthermore, one must add the number of former military internees that represents hundreds of thousands of men immersed in the development of German production, as other tens of thousands of Italians that already were in the Reich as free workers in factories and in fields.

Given these facts, the Italians that live in the territory of the Social Republic have the right to raise their heads and demand that their effort be equally evaluated by all of the components of the Tripartite Pact.

We heard, of yesterday's Eden's declarations on the casualties Britain suffered in Greece's defense. For three years Italy has inflicted heavy damages to the British, and, above all, has endured enormous sacrifices both in assets and in blood.

It is not enough.

In 1945 Italy's participation in the war shall reach a greater development through the progressive reinforcement of our military organizations, entrusted to the faith and proven experience of that soldier that holds the rank of Italy's field marshal, Rodolfo Graziani.

During the turmoil transition period from autumn to winter, 1943 more or less autonomous military groups emerged around men that, with their past and their prestige, have known how to recruit the first combatants' nucleus. It was the time of the individual enrolment of battalions, of regiments and of specialists. The old commanders sounded the bugle call. It was an excellent initiative, above all from a moral point of view. But modern warfare demands unity, and we walk towards it.

I dare to say that the Italians, whatever their thoughts may be, shall feel happy in the day in which all of the Republic's armed forces are to be integrated in a sole organism and a sole police force is to be constituted, and that both, articulated accordingly to their respective function, may live intimately identified with the climate and the spirit of Fascism and of the Republic, since that in a war such as this, that has assumed a "political" war feature, the apolitical spirit is meaningless, and by all means, is completely overrun.

Revolutionary Fascism

One thing is "politics", that is to say the convinced and fanatic adhesion to the idea that one fights for, other is the soldier's political activity, that constrained by orders and by the fulfillment of his duty, he does not even have time enough to explain, given that his politics should be restricted to his readiness to combat and to give the example in whatever situation, both in peace as in war.

In 15th of September the Fascist National Party was converted into the Fascist Republican Party. Then there were no shortness of elements that opportunistically motivated or perhaps in a state of mental confusion asked whether it would not had been more strategic to eliminate the word "Fascist" to replace it by the one of "Republic". I refused then, as I would today, this useless and vile suggestion.

There would have been an error and a vile thing to lower our flag, consecrated with so much blood, to therefore almost smuggle those ideas that nowadays constitute the watchword in all of the continent's battling. Being nothing more than a convenience flag formality, we would have lost face before our adversaries and, above all, before ourselves.

Naming ourselves once more, as always, as Fascists and consecrating ourselves to Fascism's cause like we have done since 1919 until today, and as we will continue to do tomorrow, after the past events we wanted to give a new impulse and reach to the action both in the political as in the social field.

Truthfully, more than a new reach, we should say more precisely: a return to the original positions.

It is an historical fact that Fascism was, until 1922, tendentiously Republican, and the motives by which the 1922 insurrection respected the Monarchy are obvious.

From a social point of view, the Republican Fascist program is no more than the logical continuation of the splendid years reaching from the Labor Chart to the Empire's conquest. Nature does not develop in leaps, nor does economy.

We needed to establish the basis, with Syndical laws and Corporative organisms, to set about the ulterior phase of Socialization. Already since the first meeting of the Ministers Cabinet in the 27th of September, 1943, have I declared that "the Republic should be Unitarian in the political field and decentralized in the administrative one, as well as having a most higher social accent with the purpose of dealing with the social question at least in its most important aspects, such as to establish the place, the function, the responsibility of labor in a truly modern national society".

In that same meeting, I gave the first step towards the widest national concordance possible, announcing that the government would not adopt rigorous measures against the Antifascist elements.

During the month of October, I elaborated and reviewed what in the Italian political history is nominated as the "Manifest of Verona", which established in a few points, sufficiently explicit, the program not only of the Party, but of the Republic. This has taken place exactly on the 4th of November, two months after the constitution of the Fascist Republican Party. In the FRP's national assembly's manifest, after paying tribute to the memory of the fallen for the Fascist cause and reaffirming as a supreme demand the continuation of the struggle at the Tripartite powers side and the reorganization of the armed forces, were laid out the 18 points of the program. Let us see what has been done, what has not been done, and, above all, why has it not been done.

The "Manifest" started off by demanding the summoning of a Constitutive [Assembly], specifying the members that were to compose it, so it would be - as mentioned - "the synthesis of all the Nation's values."

Well, the Constitutive [Assembly] was never summoned. This guideline has not yet been fulfilled. Nor can it be achieved before the end of the war. I want to say clearly on to thee that I have thought to be superfluous to summon a Constitutive [Assembly] while the Republic's territory could not be considered in any way as a definitive one, due to the development of military operations. I thought as premature the creation of a true state of rights in the plenitude if its institutions as long as we didn't possess the armed force to sustain it. A state not disposing of armed forces is everything but a state.

The "Manifest" stated that no citizen could be detained for more than seven days without a court order. This has not always been the case. The causes must be searched in the plurality of police organisms, both ours and of our allies, and in the "outlaws" activity that have escalated this problems into a civil war made of reprisals and counter reprisals. Antifascism has

Revolutionary Fascism

unclenched the speculation upon such episodes, exaggerating and generalizing it.

I must declare in the most explicit way that such methods deeply disgust me, even in an episodically way. The state, as such, cannot adopt methods that degrade it. From centuries ago, one talks about the Talion law. Well, it's all about a law, not an arbitrary act and, even less, personal.

Mazzini - the inflexible apostle of the Republican idea - sent, in the dawn of the Roman Republic in 1849, a commissar to Ancona to teach the Jacobins that it was licit to fight against the Papists; but not to kill them outside the law or to requisition - as one would say today - the silvery from their homes. If someone was to do so, in possession of the Party's membership card, he would be twice a criminal.

No severity is too excessive, if one wants that the Party - as it can be read in the "Verona Manifest" - truly be a front of combatants and believers, an organism of absolute political purity, and a worthy custodian of the revolutionary idea. A high personification of this kind of Fascist was comrade Resega, who we remember today with profound emotion in the occasion of the first anniversary of his death, caused by enemy hand.

Being that, through the constitution of the Black Brigades, the Party is being converted into a "combatant's front", the Verona guidelines have the character of a dogmatic and sacred compromise. In its 5th article, in which it was established that by no compromise or influence should the Party's insignia be compromised, the problem that I shall nominate as the cooperation of other elements as far as it concerns the Republic was solved. In my telegram XXII, dating of 10th of March, to the provincial leaders, such a formula would be presented in a more detailed way. From then on all discussion on the issue of the party's plurality is an anachronistic one.

Historically - in the various forms that the Republic has assumed among different peoples - there are many Republics of totalitarian type, and therefore with a sole party. I shall not quote the most totalitarian among them, the one of the Soviets, but I shall remember one that enjoys the fondness of the high priests of the Democratic gospel: the Turkish Republic, supported by a sole Party - the [Republican] People's Party - and a sole youth organization - the People's Houses.

In a given moment of the Italian historic evolution, the presence of other groups, that, as it is stated in Art. 3 of the "Verona Manifest", exercise the right to examine and responsibly criticize the acts of the public administration, may have fecund results, outside the Party, the sole responsible of the state's global direction. Groups that, given their loyal, integral and unreserved acceptance of the trinomial Italy, Republic, Socialization, have the responsibility of examining the government's and local entities guidelines, of surveying the orders application methods and the persons that hold public offices that, as such, must be held accountable of their actions before the citizen in its quality of soldier/worker/taxpayer.

The Verona's assembly has established its foreign policy guidelines, in Art. 8. It was simply stated that the essential goal of the Republic's foreign policy is "the unity, the independence and the territorial integrity of the Fatherland in its maritime and alpine limits designated by nature, by bloody sacrifice and by History".

As to the territorial unity I refuse - knowing Sicily and the Sicilian brothers - to take seriously the so-called separatist attempts of the despicable enemy's mercenaries. It may well be that this separatism has another reason: that the brothers from Sicily want to part from Bonomi's Italy to rejoin the Italian Republic.

I'm profoundly convinced that - in spite of all the fighting and once liquidated the criminal phenomenon of the outlaws - the moral unity of tomorrow's Italians will be infinitely stronger than that of those of yesterday, given that it shall be cemented upon exceptional sufferings that haven't spared a single family. And when, trough moral unity, a people's soul is kept safe, it also safeguards its territorial integrity and political independence.

In this point, a few words about Europe are in order. I don't want to detain myself in asking what is Europe, where it starts and where it ends from a geographical, historical, moral and economic point of view; nor do I ask myself, today, if a unification attempt may know a better result than the previous ones. That would take me too far. I confine myself to say that the constitution of an European community is desirable and inclusively possible, but I must declare in the most explicit way that we do not feel like as Italians because we are European, but that we feel like Europeans because we are Italian. This is not a subtle distinction but a fundamental one. Being as it may that the nation is the result of millions of families that have a physiognomy of their own and that possess a common national denominator, each nation should join the European community as a well defined entity, so to prevent that the community would sink into Socialist Internationalism or vegetate in generic and equivocal Cosmopolitism with a Jewish and Masonic brand.

Meanwhile that such "Verona Manifest" points have been set aside by a succession of military events, in the economical-social field more concrete realizations have been carried out.

In this aspect, the innovations acquire a radical character. Points 11, 12 and 13 are fundamental. Precised in the "new economic structure of the nation premise" its practical application can be found in the law on Socialization. The interest that it has aroused in the world has been truly a great one, and today, everywhere, including in Italy, dominated and tortured by the Anglo-Americans, all of the political programs contain the Socialization guidelines.

The workers, more or less skeptical at the beginning, ended up by understanding its importance. Its effective realization is on the move. In other times, its rhythm would have been quicker. But, now, the seed has been sown. No matter what may occur, this seed is destined to germinate. it's the principle that inaugurates what I have I foretold eight years ago, here, in Milan, before 150,000 persons that were acclaiming me, the "labor century" in which the worker rises from its economic/moral condition of wage-earner to assume one of producer, a directly interested part in the economy's development and in the nation's welfare.

Fascist Socialization is the logical and rational solution that avoids, the economy's burocratization through a state Totalitarianism in one hand, overcoming, by the other, the Liberal economy's individualism that was an effective instrument of progress in the beginnings of the Capitalist economy, but that today must not be considered as a solution in accordance with the demands of the national community's "social" character.

By means of the Socialization the best elements from the working classes shall prove themselves.

I am decided to proceed in this direction.

I have entrusted two sectors to the working classes: the local administration and the supplying. These sectors, of the utmost importance in today's circumstances, are already in the hands of the workers. These ones must demonstrate, and I hope that they will do so, their specific preparation and civic conscience.

As you can see, we have indeed achieved something during these twelve months in the midst of increasing and incredible difficulties, due to the objective circumstances of the war and to the dull opposition of elements sold out to the enemy, as well as to the extreme moral apathy in which the [past] events have plunged many sectors of the people.

In these last times the situation has improved. The opportunists, those who were waiting for the Anglo-Americans, are fewer every day. The events that are occurring in Bonomi's Italy have disillusioned them. Everything that the Anglo-Americans have promised has amounted to nothing but a miserable propagandistic scam.

I believe to be right when I say that in the Po valley, not only [people] do not desire, but in deed fear, the Anglo-Saxons arrival; they want nothing to do with a government that by having a Togliatti in its vice-presidency would arouse the reactionary forces in the north, plutocratic and dynastical, mainly these last ones, plainly protected by England.

How ridiculous are those Republicans that do not want the Republic due to the mere fact that it has been proclaimed by Mussolini and on the other hand let themselves be subjugated by the Monarchy, wanted by Churchill! This demonstrates in an irrefutable way that the Savoy monarchy serves the Great Britain's policy and not the one of Italy.

There is no doubt whatsoever that the fall of Rome constitutes a culminating date in the history of the war. General Alexander has declared that it was necessary, in the eve of the disembarkation in France, a victory that would be linked to a name of grandeur - and there is no greater and universal name than the one of Rome - and, that with it, an atmosphere of optimism would be created.

The Anglo-Americans entered Rome in the 5th of June. In the following day, the 6th, the first "allied" sections disembarked in the coast of Normandy, between the rivers Vire and Orne. The following months have been extremely tough, above all in the fronts where the Reich soldiers were, and still are, committed into the fight.

Revolutionary Fascism

Germany has called all of hers human reserves to the ranks, with a total mobilization directed by Goebbels and with the creation of the Volkssturm. Only a people such as the German, gathered around the Führer, could endure such an enormous pressure, only an army such as the National Socialist could quickly overcome the crisis of the 20th of July and continue to struggle on in the four corners of the world with the exceptional tenacity and valor recognized even by the enemy himself.

There was a moment in which the conquests of Brussels and Paris, the unconditional surrendering of Romania, Finland and Bulgaria gave way to such a state of euphoria that - giving credit to the war correspondents - one would believe that by this Christmas the war would have been practically over with the triumphal entry of the Allies in Berlin.

In the period of euphoria that we have alluded to, the new German weapons, that have been improperly called "secret", have been devaluated and disdained.

Many believe that due to the use of such weapons, in a given moment, as if one was to ring a bell, the war would suddenly end, this trust in a miracle, more than naïf, must be considered harmful. We are not dealing with secret weapons, but with "new weapons" that - needless to say - are only secret until they are used in combat. That such weapons exist is known, through bitter experience, by the English; that these first ones shall be replaced by others, I can knowingly claim so; that these ones have such an efficiency that they may, from the start, come about to re-establish an equilibrium and shortly after allowed to resume the initiative is, within the limit of human forecasts, a thing almost certain and not far.

Nothing more understandable than impatience, after five years of war, but these are instruments in which science, technique, the experience and the training of each soldier and of the units are mandatory. It is indeed true that the series of surprises is not infinite, and that thousands of German scientists work, day and night, to increase Germany's potential warlike power. Meanwhile the German resistance is getting more solid and many of the illusions that the enemy propaganda harbored have already fallen. None, whatsoever, debilitation of the German people's moral, fully conscious that it's physical existence and its future as a race is at stake; none, whatsoever, sign of a revolution, not even of restlessness among the millions and millions of foreign workers, in spite of the appeals and proclamations of the American generalissimo. A most eloquent rate of the nation's spirit is the percentage of volunteers in the last draft, very close to the total number of the enrolled. Germany is able to resist and to disrupt the enemy's plans.

To minimize the lost of territories, once conquered and maintained at blood cost, is not an intelligent tactic, nor, nevertheless, is it the war's objective to conquer or to hold territories, but the destruction of enemy forces and, therefore, the end of hostilities.

Today the German armed forces not only are not destroyed, but they find themselves in a phase of crescent development and power.

If one is to examine the situation from a political point of view, this last period of 1944, has witnessed the maturing of some interesting events and states of mind without exaggerating, one can say that the political situation today is not favorable to the Allies. Mainly in America and England, where currents of opinion contrary to the unconditional surrendering demands have arise. The Casablanca's formula means the death of millions of young men, since it prolongs the war indefinitely: peoples like the German and the Japanese shall not surrender bound and gagged to an enemy in whose plans is inscribed the total annihilation of the countries that form the Tripartite.

This explains the cold shower that Mr. Churchill has been forced to give to his compatriots, prorogating the date of conflict's end until the summer of 1945 for Europe and 1947 for Japan.

The Soviet ambassador in Rome, Potemkin, once told me: "The First World War Bolshevized Russia, the Second will Bolshevize Europe".

This prophecy shall not be fulfilled; however, if this should come to pass, all of the responsibility would befall on Great Britain.

Politically, Albion is already eliminated. The Russian armies are now between the Vistula and the Danube, that is to say, on half of Europe. The Communist parties, better said, the parties that act upon the orders of field marshal Stalin, are in power in most of the countries of the West.

What does it mean the word "liberation" in Belgium, Italy and Greece? The information's that we receive daily enlighten us: misery, desperation and civil war. The "liberated" Greeks that await their English "liberators" are but Russian Communists that await their British Conservatives.

Revolutionary Fascism

In sight of this panorama, the English policy had to adopt a defensive attitude. First of all, liquidating in a dramatic and bloody fashion - like in Athens - the "Partisan" movements that constitute the operational and combatant wing of the Far Left, of Bolshevism; Secondly, supporting the Democratic forces that refuse the totalitarianism which finds its most refined expression in Soviet Russia.

Churchill has waved the Anti-Communist banner in the most categorical way in his last speech before the House of Commons, but this does not pleases Stalin. Great Britain wants to reserve Western Europe as a Democratic influence zone, and does not want that it may be, in any case, contaminated by Communism.

But this Churchill's "frond" cannot reach but a certain limit, given that, if not so, the great field marshal of the Kremlin could become suspicious.

Churchill wanted that the Western European influence zone reserved to Democracy were to be protected by a pact between France, England, Belgium, Holland and Norway, oriented against, first of all, Germany and eventually against Russia.

The Stalin-de Gaulle agreement has suffocated this idea at birth, launched - accordingly to the instructions of London - by the Belgian Spaak. The game has failed, and Churchill can do no other than - as the English put it - to eat his own hat, and, thinking in the Russians entry in the Mediterranean and in the Russian pressure on Iran, he must ask [himself] if the Casablanca policy has not, in reality, constituted a policy of failure to the "old and poor England".

Placed in the middle of two military colossi, the one of the West and the one of the East, by its insolent and insatiable cousins from the other side of the ocean and by the never-ending Eurasians, Great Britain sees the future of its empire in peril, that is to say, its destiny. That the "political" relations among the Allies are not very good is demonstrated by the tiresome preparations for the Three's next meeting.

Erik Norling

Let us now talk about the remote and [yet] close Japan. It is incontrovertible that the empire of the rising sun will never surrender and that it will fight until victory. In these last months, the Japanese armed forces have achieved great successes. The units of the so proclaimed disembarkation in the Leyte island - one among the hundreds of islands that form the Philippine archipelago -, disembarkation that was carried out for electoral purposes, are, after two months, [stalled] almost in the same place.

Japan's will and spirit has been demonstrated by the death volunteers. They are not just a few dozens, but tens of thousands of young men that act upon this slogan: "for each aircraft, an enemy ship". And they do it. In view of this over-human and heroic decision, one understands the attitude of some American circles that ask themselves if it would not have been better for the United States if Roosevelt had fulfilled his promise made to the American mothers that no soldier would be sent to fight and die overseas. The president lied, as usual in all of the democracies.

For us, Italians of the Republic, it is a motive of pride to have by our side comrades so faithful and polite - the Tenno's soldiers, mariners and aviators - that with their epic deeds are the object of the world's admiration.

Now I ask of thee: the Italians' good seed, of those sane Italians - the best - that see death in the service of the fatherland as eternal live, should be considered as already extinguished? Was there not, during the war, an aviator that being unable to shoot down an enemy aircraft, dived against it? Do you remember his name? He was an humble sergeant: Dall'Oro.

In 1935, when England wanted to trap us in our sea, I've picked up its challenging glove and had more than 400,000 legionnaires parading before his British majesty's ships anchored in the Mediterranean harbors. It was then that in Rome were constituted the death squadrons. I must say, truth be said, that the first to enlist was the air force commander. Well, if tomorrow should be proven necessary to reconstitute these squadrons, if it were to be necessary to demonstrate that in our veins still runs the blood of the Roman legionnaires, would my appeal fall into empty ears?

We want to defend the Po valley, with tooth and nail if need be; we want that the Po valley remains Republican in the expectation that the whole of Italy shall also become it.

Revolutionary Fascism

In the day in which the Po valley were to be occupied by the enemy, the destiny of the whole nation would be compromised. But I feel it; I see it that tomorrow would emerge a kind of organization, armed and irresistible, that would rend the invaders lives practically impossible. We shall convert the entire Po valley into a sole Athens.

It is evident, for all that I have just said to thee, that the enemy coalition not only hasn't won, but that it shall not win.

The monstrous alliance between Plutocracy and Bolshevism has been able to unclench its barbaric war thus perpetrating an enormous crime that sacrifices a multitude of innocents and destroys that which the European civilization has created in twenty centuries. But it shall not succeed with its barbarism to annihilate the eternal spirit extolled by such monuments. Our absolute faith in victory is not supported by motives of a subjective and sentimental order, but on positive and determinant elements. If we were to doubt our victory, we should also question the existence of the One that regulates, accordingly to justice, men's faith.

When we, soldiers of the Republic, are to establish contact with the Italians from the other side of the Apennine, we shall experience a pleasant surprise to find Fascism even more alive than when we left it. The disillusion, the misery and the political and moral abjection does not burst only in the old phrase: "we were better of when we were worst", but revolt is already spreading throughout Palermo, Catania, Otranto, in Rome itself and all throughout "liberated" Italy.

The Italian people, south of the Apennine has its soul filled with nostalgia. The enemy operation by one hand, and the bestial prosecution of the government by the other, do no more than to foment the Fascist movement. The task of eliminating its external symbols was easy; but the one of suppressing the idea, is impossible.

The six anti-Fascist parties haste to proclaim that Fascism is dead, precisely because they feel it [so much] alive. Millions of Italians compare past and present days; of days gone by when the fatherland's flag was waving from the Alps to the Equator, and the Italian was one of the most respected peoples of Earth.

Erik Norling

There isn't a sole Italian that doesn't feel his heart beat in his chest when hearing an African name, listening to the hymn that accompanied the Mediterranean legions to the Red Sea, or in the sight of a colonial helmet. There are millions of Italians that from 1929 to 1939 have lived what can be defined as the fatherland's Epopee. These Italians still exist, they suffer and they believe and are able to close the ranks to march once again to reconquest all that was lost between the Libyan dunes and the frontiers of Ethiopia, guarded [as it is] by thousands and thousands of fallen, the blossom of enumerable Italian families that haven't, nor can, forget it.

One can already foresee the reconquest annunciating signs, above all here, in pioneer and forefront Milan that the enemy so savagely stroke but that hasn't been able to make it bow down even in the slightest of ways.

Comrades, dear Milanese comrades!

It is Milan that must and will give the men, the weapons, the will and the sign for the rescue!

XI
Chronology: the 600 days of the RSI

1943

24/25th July Destitution of Mussolini by a Grand Council session.

25th July The king, Vittorio Emmanuelle III, orders the arrest of Mussolini. Badoglio appointed as head of the government.

3rd September Secret armistice of Cassabile. The 8th British army disembarks in Calabria

8th September The armistice is made public. German countermeasures.

9th September Allied disembarkations in Taranto and Salerno.

10th September Hitler orders the occupation of Italy and its division in two zones.

12th September Mussolini is liberated from the Grand Sasso.

14th September Meeting between Mussolini-Hitler in the Wolf's Lair.

18th September Mussolini speech to the Italians from Radio Munich.

23rd September constitution of the government of the ISR.

27th September First session of the ISR government in Rocca delle Camínate.

1st of October - Speech of field marshal Graziani in the Lyrical Theatre of Rome. The Germans evacuate Naples.

8th of October - Mussolini moves his government to Gargnano next to the Garda lake.

13th of October - Badoglio's government declares war on Germany.

27th of October - Second session of the ISR government.

8th of November - the 8th British army crosses the river Sangro.

11th of November - Creation of the exceptional special tribunal and of the provincial exceptional tribunals.

14th of November - Verona Congress.

20th of November - The creation of the National Republican Guard is made public.

21st of November - Field marshal Kesselring assumes the defense of Italy in his quality of commander of the Southwest front.

25th of November - Third session of the ISR government.

1st of December - The new state assumes the denomination of Italian Social Republic.

2nd/3rd of December - the Germans bombard Bari. They destroy 90 merchant ships.

16th of December - Fourth session of the ISR government.

29th of December - The 8th British army conquers Ortona.

1944

8th/10th of January - Verona's criminal procedure against the Fascist's that voted against the Duce in the Grand Counsel Session.

11th of January - Ciano, De Bono, Marienlli, Pareschi and Gottardi are executed by firing squad in Verona.

13th of January - Fifth session of the ISR government. Announcing of the Socialization.

22nd of January - American disembarkations in Anzio and Neptune.

24th of January - The first battle of Monte Cassino begins.

12th of February - Sixth session of the ISR government.

15th/18th of February - Second battle of Monte Cassino.

15th of February - The Allies destroy the Monte Cassino's monastery through bombing.

16th/21st of February - The Anzio's counteroffensive fails.

29th of February - Second German counteroffensive in Anzio, equally fails by the 1st of March.

9th of March - Creation of the Feminine Auxiliary Service (FAS).

11th of March - Seventh session of the ISR Ministers Cabinet.

15th/24th of March - Third battle of Monte Cassino. Allied defeat.

23rd of March - Assault, in Rome's Via Rasella, against a Tyrolese police unit.

24th of March - Ardeatine pits reprisal in Rome.

29th of March - The Republican aviation shots down 14 Allied bombers.

15th of April - The philosopher Giovanni Gentile is murdered by Communists in Florence.

18th of April - Eight session of the ISR government.

22nd/23rd of April - Meeting between Hitler and Mussolini in the Clessheim castle, near Salzburg.

Revolutionary Fascism

24th of April - The Duce visit's the San Marco division in the training facilities of Grafenwöhr.

12th of May - Allied offensive against the 10th German army in Garigolíano.

17th of May - The German paratroopers evacuate Monte Cassino.

24th of May - The admirals Campione and Mascherpa are shot down by firing squad after being sentenced to death by the Special Tribunal.

25th of May - General German retrieval from the Adriatic to the Tyrrhenian Sea.

4th of June - Rome falls in the hands of the Allies.

4th/5th of June - The Republican aviation attacks Gibraltar.

6th of June - Allied disembarkation in Normandy.

19th of June - The Allies conquer Perugia.

2nd/3rd of July - The Germans evacuate Siena.

15th/22nd of July - Mussolini travels to Germany.

18th of July - The Allies occupy Ancona.

22nd of July - Attempt on Hitler. Last meeting between Hitler and Mussolini.

25th of July - The RFP militarizes. Pavolini announces the creation of the Black Brigades.

2nd of August - The field marshal Graziani assumes the command of the Liguria army corps.

4th of August - The German paratroopers evacuate the south of Florence. The Fascists decide to offer a desperate resistance.

10th of August - The German troops retreat from Florence.

15th of August - The Allies disembark on the Mediterranean French coast.

21st of August - San Marino declares war on Germany.

1st of September - The 10th German army resists the Allied offensive in Rimini.

2nd of September - The Germans evacuate Pisa.

15th of September - The Jonick islands are evacuated by the Germans.

21st of September - British units conquer Rimini.

12th of October - Eleventh session of the ISR government.

26th of October - The Allies fail in overcoming the Apennine's defense line in order to reach Bologna.

16th of November - Twelfth session of the ISR government.

5th of December - Ravena is evacuated by the Germans.

9th of December - Thirteenth of the ISR government.

16th of December - Arden's offensive. Mussolini speech at the Milanese Lyrical Theatre.

16th/17th of December - The 8th British army conquers Faenza.

26th/30th of December - Successful Italian-German offensive in the Cerchio valley.

29th of December - All kinds of lodging facilities are transformed in collective canteens.

1945

19th of January - Fourteenth session of the ISR government.

22nd of January - Fiat is Socialized.

24th of January - Pavolini visits the Italian units in Venetia Giulia.

1st of February - Socialization is extended to other companies.

14th of February - Is announced the creation of the Socialist National Republican Grouping.

21st of February - Mussolini orders the destitution of Buffarini Guidi.

8th of March - Secrete conversations between General Wolff and the Allies.

12th of March - In Rome, the criminal procedure against the Fascist hierarchs comes to an end. Anfuso is sentenced to death in absentia.

15th of March - Sixteenth session of the ISR Ministers Cabinet.

9th of April - Beginning of the 8th British army grand offensive on the Eastern sector of the Italian front.

14th of April - The 5th American army initiates the offensive in the Western sector.

16th of April - Seventeenth section of the ISR government.

18th of April - Mussolini arrives to Milan.

25th of April - The Allies cross the Po, occupying Mantova, Reggio and Parma. Mussolini and his government abandon Milan.

27th of April - Mussolini is captured by the Partisans. The French occupy Ventimiglia e Bordighera.

Revolutionary Fascism

28th of April - Mussolini is assassinated in Giulino de Mezzegra. In Dongo the Fascist hierarchs are shot.

29th of April - The capitulation of the German forces in Italy is signed in Caserta.

30th of April - Hitler's suicide. The Americans occupy Turin.

2nd of May - The German surrendering in Italy, to take place at 2pm, is publicly announced.

www.ingramcontent.com/pod-product-compliance
Lightning Source LLC
Chambersburg PA
CBHW032135040426
42449CB00005B/254